BOKO HARAM
&
THE AGENDA OF A FAILED NIGERIA STATE

RICHARD SIMONS, Ph.D.

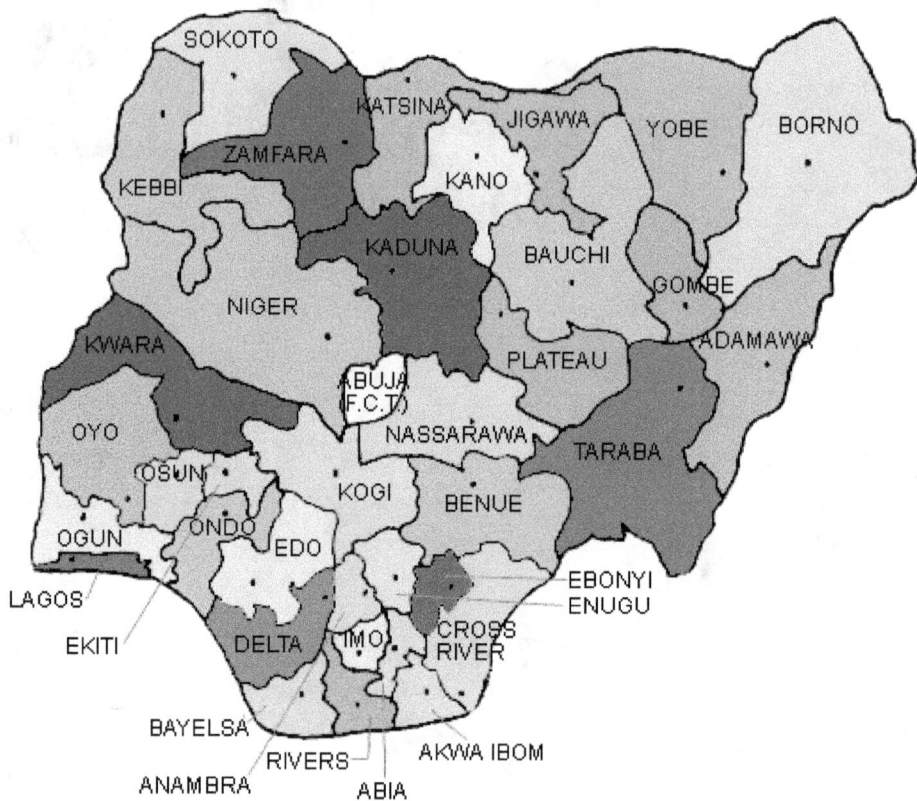

Any government that supports, protects or harbors terrorists is complicit in the murder of the innocent and equally guilty of terrorist crimes.[1]
                              - George W. Bush

Human Rights are not only violated by terrorism, repression and assassination, but also by unfair economic structures that create huge inequalities.[2]
                              - Pope Francis

No act of terror can match the strength or the character of our country.[3]
                              - President Barack Obama

To all victims of terror - their families, relatives and friends.

Prologue

Since Nigeria gained her independence from Britain in 1960, the country has witnessed political upheavals, sectarian violence along ethnic and religious lines. These incidents were mostly unpredictable; none including the Nigeria civil war has threatened the internal security of Nigeria than Boko Haram's terrorism. Maiduguri in Northern Nigeria is the base of the terror group –Boko Haram. In Hausa language, Boko Haram means, "Western education is sinful." The group has its goal to Islamize Nigeria, to occupy Northern and Central states by ensuring that Nigeria is a failed state with no federal authority to stop its Jihadist's march to Western targets - cities in Europe and the United States.

However, pundits have expressed disdain over a culture in Nigeria that indirectly motivates violence by the lack of any prosecution of perpetrators of violence such as Boko Haram leaders, some politicians and religious leaders allegedly supporting the terror group. These individuals and their accomplices, in spite of deaths of more than 13, 000 Nigerians and foreign workers worry Nigerians who see these individuals that the president of Nigeria, Jonathan Goodluck claims some supporters of the terror group were in his cabinet work free on the streets.

The incidents of violence committed by Boko

Haram are everywhere and documented including the April 14, 2014 kidnapping of 276 Chibok schoolgirls. Pundits opined that the lackadaisical attitude of the government and its failure to prosecute these perpetrators of violence motivate others to repeat the crime.

Prior to Boko Haram's emergence, the Federal Government pundits argue that after decades of conflicts in the name of sectarian violence witnessed in Nigeria continue to repeat because the government has also not been able to establish a national program to address the relationship between more than 250 tribes and religious groups merged together under the British amalgamation project in 1914. The amalgamation, experts also claim exacerbates the ethnic and religious problems facing Nigeria in the 21st century. It is this diversity gap that groups such as Boko Haram and other religious and political extremists take advantage to destabilize Nigeria.

Majority of Nigerians has advocated for a Sovereign National Conference. The clarion call was answered by President Goodluck administration in 2014 after decades of frustrations from politicians that never wanted the conference to take place. The Sovereign National Conference sat in Abuja and came up with report that its contents are yet to be made public (and may be unlikely made public because like the controversy leading to the eventual siting of the committee, there is still divided opinions and mistrust among tribes about the objectivity of the committee and its report).

Nigerians advocating for the National Sovereign Conference (and they were from various ethnic groups and religious backgrounds) strongly believed that Nigerians are long overdue for coming together to work out constitutional framework that will address issues about the dimensions of relationships among its diverse ethnic groups. Nigerians wanted the Sovereign National Conference to look into how Nigerians could live harmoniously together amidst their socio-political, cultural and religious differences that have been the barriers to peace and unity in the country. The neglect of these barriers, as witnessed from the turn of events in the last 54 years since Nigeria gained her independence in 1960 from Britain, have fueled conflicts, and thus provided distractions to national cohesion needed for Nigeria to reach its economic potentials.

While pundits have attributed the killings to sentiments motivated by politicians who use religion to camouflage their agenda, others have identified the problems with Nigeria that exacerbate sectarian violence as stemming from Nigeria's weak foundation. They are implying that the constitution that never addressed such issues as religion (sharia) and politics, rights of Nigerians to live and own land in some parts of the country among other major problems that the constitution did not address. Some religious and political leaders have exploited in the past these weaknesses by their proxy or themselves motivating criminal acts and got away with them.

However, before September 11, 2001 in the United States when terrorists flew and rammed their hijacked planes into the World Trade Center killing more than 3000 Americans and other citizens of the world, not much information about Osama Bin Ladin, Ayman al-Zawahiri, Al-Qaida, and their African connections were available. Osama Bin Laden came to World's attention following the bombings of the United States Embassies in the East African capitals of Dar es Salaam, Tanzania, and Nairobi, Kenya on August 7, 1998. The attacks were later identified as the handiwork of local members of the Egyptian Islamic Jihad and masterminded by Fazul Abdullah Mohammed, killed hundreds of Africans, and Osama Bin Ladin was placed on America's Most Wanted list.

The US Embassies' attacks in Kenya and Tanzania also opened the eyes of the world about the existence of terror cells in Africa that hitherto were not in the headlines as policy decisions on the fight against extremists were focused on the Middle East. With the bombing of the World Trade Center complex in New York on September 11, 2001, and the search for Osama Bin Ladin, and his African connections and network began to emerge. Also, revealed was the infiltration of Al-Qaida into Africa, and the level of military-style training the group provides for would-be terrorists.

Kenya witnessed yet another terror attack. Terrorists from Somalia tossed grenades and fired assault rifles inside Nairobi's shopping mall. About 39 people were killed, and 150 wounded in the incident. Somalia's Al Qaeda-linked Shebaab group claimed responsibility for the attack. Kenya's president Uhuru Kenyatta in a national TV broadcast to the Kenyan people disclosed his close family members were among the dead.[1] French and Canadian citizens were among those killed in the attack. France's president confirmed that two French women were killed. Two Canadians were also killed, including a diplomat, said the Canadian prime minister. Four American citizens were reported injured but not killed in the attack, the State Department disclosed. Somalia's Islamic extremist group al-Shabaab claimed responsibility and said the attack was retribution for Kenyan forces' 2011 push into Somalia. [2]

Associated Press reported several witnesses confirming that prior to the attack the al-Qaida-linked gunmen were asking the victims that they came across if they were Muslim: Those who responded in the affirmative were set free while non-Muslims were held hostage. Kenyan security sources also confirmed that the vests found with Al-Qaida linked gunmen on September 21, 2003 were similar to those used by jihadists that killed 76 people in Uganda. The victims were TV viewers who gathered to watch the soccer World Cup finals on TV in July 2010. Al-Shabaab claimed responsibility for the bombing. It revealed the attack was in retaliation for Uganda's participation in the African Union's peacekeeping mission in Somalia.

In Nigeria, many terror attacks could be traced to Boko Haram, even before it adopted its current name. For instance, the November 2002 Miss World pageant was aborted as a result of rioting by "religious fundamentalists" that were against the hosting of the beauty contest in Nigeria. The leaders and actors in the rioting saw hosting of Miss World pageant on Nigeria soil as "sacrilegious" and any nudity or exposure of women's body against sharia law; the connection between the ideology that led to the rioting parallels the ideology that Boko Haram advocates toward the Islamization project of entire Nigeria. Like the attack on fans watching World Cup games in Uganda, which al-Shabaab claimed responsibility, In Nigeria on June 1, 2014, fans watching soccer match in Mubi, Northeastern Nigeria were attacked when a bomb was detonated on the stand they were watching television. More than 40 fans were killed. The bombing incident came barely a week Nigeria soccer team, the Giant Eagles is scheduled to play the United States national team at Jacksonville, in preparation for the World cup soccer in August in Brazil.[3]

The "rioters" in 2002 claimed that the scheduling of the Miss World pageant that promoted "Western culture" was fixed to coincide with the Ramadan festival known in the Muslim community as the Eid al-Fitr, the end of the fasting period. Opposition within the Muslim groups in Nigeria advocated that the pageant be cancelled or moved to another date, but radical groups wanted the event out of the country. Despite the event organizers effort to shift the date of the event forward in respect to the Muslim festival, the protests against hosting the pageant in Nigeria continued.

The rioters, supported by their clerics, extremists insisted that the pageant must not be held. The rioting broke out of control when *ThisDay* newspaper columnist, Isioma Daniel's comments involving the Islamic prophet Muhammad sparked major religious riots and caused a fatwa to be issued on her life. The comment triggered violent religious riots that left more than 200 dead and 1,000 injured, with 11,000 people made homeless. *ThisDay's* offices in Kaduna were razed in spite of apology and retraction of the comment on the front page of the newspaper. The protesters mainly Muslim youths, roamed on the streets unknown that behind the protest were radical groups. From Kaduna, Kano, and Abuja the protest went on. Miss World 2002 was eventually cancelled and moved to London as organizers feared for the worse.

More than ten years after *ThisDay* newspaper was razed, and Ms. Daniel escaped to Europe after Fatwa was declared on her, evidences are emerging that Boko Haram was founded in Maiduguri when the Muslims rioters aborted the Miss World pageant. The group referred in 2013 to a confrontation with *ThisDay* in 2001. In a YouTube video posted online, Boko Haram warned the media of reporting subjectively about Boko Haram's operations. They accused the media of working with the federal government by providing the authorities with logistics about the terror group.

Through its leader, the terrorist group warned that the fate of *ThisDay* Newspaper in 2002 would soon face the media in Nigeria especially in the North if the media do not desist from their subjective reporting of the terror group. They also warned that the media should have learned lessons on what to and what not to report to avoid repeating the experiences of *ThisDay*. In essence, media would face the same consequences if it does not report the activities of the group 'objectively.

In 2012, media reported that the leader of the group was killed following gunfire exchange with the security agents that had gone to his hideout to arrest him. It was headline news that Boko Haram declared as a propaganda that supported the federal government's war against the terror group. Referencing the *ThisDay* attack from 2002 and using the experience to threaten Nigeria media in 2012 showed a connection between the two especially as the group claimed that it masterminded the attack on *ThisDay*.

Since 2009 when Boko Haram leader, Mohammed Yusuf was killed during a clash between militants and security forces, the terrorists have killed more than

12, 000 Nigerians and foreigners. Human Rights Watch released a report revealing that Boko Haram insurgents had slaughtered 2,053 people in an estimated 95 attacks during the first six months of 2014. The killings were part of widespread attacks on civilian targets in over 70 towns and villages in northeastern Nigeria, in the federal capital, Abuja, and Lagos.[4] However, the casualties mostly were security agents and Christians, mainly of Igbo extractions from Southeastern Nigeria. Boko Haram has also extended its terror to national institutions – State Security Services, the police force and the military; it has also killed foreign workers including Germans, British, North Korean doctors and kidnapped French families on vacation in Nigeria. The terror group has also not spared Northern leaders who criticized members or the group.

With such high death rates, it seems there is no end in sight to this war now that Boko Haram's splinter groups have emerged. Smaller al-Qaida and Boko Haram offshoots have also emerged and flourishes in Nigeria. They have their roots traced to other al-Qaida groups in North Africa, Yemen, Southern Asia, and now West Africa. They are digging up diabolical new ways to hurt their targets while focusing on their main goal of the Islamization of the spaces they occupied.

In 2002, when the Miss World pageant was cancelled and moved to London, little was known of the terror group, Boko Haram. Nevertheless, events since

2002 have begun to emerge linking the terror group's activities including deadly "riots" to Boko Haram. Also in retrospect, the aborted attacks on board Northwest Airline's Flight 253, en route from Amsterdam to Detroit and the arrest of Umar Abdul Mutallab referred as the "Underwear-Bomber," highlighted the growing radicalization of young people, not really born in Nigeria but with a Nigerian background.

The suspected terrorist in the Northwest Airline's flight helps to unravel the fears that experts on terrorism have expressed about the growing apostles of Osama Bin Ladin and their dispersion across the globe. Al-Qaeda in the Arabian Peninsula (AQAP) claimed to have organized the attack with Abdul Mutallab; they said they supplied him with a bomb and trained him. Established during the court trial and sentencing to life imprisonment without parole was Mutallab's contact with Anwar al-Awlaki, an American-born cleric and one of the known al Qaeda leaders who was killed by a drone - missile strike in Yemen on Sept. 30, 2011 in Yemen.[5]

Also on May 22, 2013 as viewers across the globe were glued to their television; they watched the horrific day-light stabbing to death of a British soldier Lee Rigby outside the Woolwich army barracks in southeast London by two British suspects identified as Michael Adebowale, 22, and Michael Olumide Adebolajo, 28, born by Nigerian parents.

All these incidents coincide with European intelligence reports that revealed Boko Haram has expanded ties with jihadist groups outside Nigeria, including al Qaeda in the Islamic Maghreb (AQIM), which operates in North African countries that border Nigeria; it becomes more important that attention is paid to African frontiers on war against terrorism. The African front is yet to receive the same attention on the war against terrorism as Afghanistan, Pakistan and Iraq. Similarly, the fall of Libya left a huge cache of state-of-the art military ammunitions and equipment in the hand of civilians some of them with ties to al Qaeda in the Islamic Maghreb (AQIM).

Before the fall of Maummar Gaddafi, Libya had 20, 000 Surface to Air missiles but after the overthrow of Gaddafi, the country was left wait only 5,000 of such missiles.[6] Where the rest have gone remains a puzzle that has not been unraveled. As many as 20,000 of the deadly Russian-made weapons disappeared from the unguarded depots, raising fears of terror attacks in the skies. "I think the probability of Al-Qaeda being able to smuggle some of stinger-like missiles out of Libya is pretty high," said former White House counterterrorism advisor Richard Clarke, now an ABC News consultant remarked.[6] This situation leaves more concerns about what terrorist groups can and cannot do with their acquired weaponry.

In this book - *Boko Haram – An Agenda of a*

Failed Nigeria State, the author revisited and examined Nigeria history traced before the amalgamation of Northern and Southern protectorate in 1914 to what is today known as Nigeria. The book also provides a background to the growth of Nigeria's religious, socio-political and economic problems. It brings into perspective, the disenchantment and loss of hope among its teaming population of youth estimated by the Nigeria Population Census 2010 as comprising more than 60 percent of the population. Why the population is an easy recruit by clerics and religious fundamentalists and now Boko Haram? The rise of Boko Haram cannot be isolated from Nigeria's politics and religion. The same manner Nigeria's ethnicity, a country divided 50-50 among Christians and Muslims population plays a role because its diversity is often exploited by politicians and religious leaders. Of course, Nigeria's weak foundation provides the environment for the thriving problems that the country encounter including sectarian violence and now terrorism that has engulfed the Northern part of Nigeria.

Chapter 1

Boko Haram –   In the Beginning

The fundamentalist group, the *Jama'atu Ahlis Sunna Lidda'awati Wal Jihad*, is also known as Boko Haram. The group name, Boko Haram in Hausa language spoken in the enclave where the group uses as its headquarters Maiduguri translates in English to, "Western education is sin." Boko Haram has referred to itself as Nigerian Taliban. It seeks to overthrow the government and replace it with its own regime based on Islamic laws.

The fundamentalist group was declared a terrorist organization in Nigeria in 2002 because of its affiliations with other Islamic groups such as the Al Qaida in Islamic Maghreb (AQIM) and the Middle East. Boko Haram's goals set to Islamize Nigeria (by using North and North-Central Nigeria as its testing grounds) and to eventually make all states in the federation administered under extreme forms of sharia laws. In essence, it has its goal of not just Islamizing Nigeria, but also set to make Nigeria a failed State, Boko Haram envisages that Nigeria will be a 'failed' state, therefore, it hopes to use the country as a base to extend its jihad to Western targets in Europe and the United States.

Boko Haram's history dated back to eras of Muslim fundamentalism in the 80's in Nigeria. Since 2009, it has metamorphosed into an independent, but extremely violent Jihadist group. The group's emergence into the limelight was traced to 2009, when Boko Haram's leader, Mohammed Yusuf was killed during a battle with federal agents.

Since then, the group has expanded its terror attacks far from targets in the North and the North Central parts of the state, to the Presidential Lodge known as Aso Rock in Abuja and beyond into other enclaves originally thought to be safe. First, Boko Haram started focusing its attacks on the military and on government targets. Not long after, it shifted to targeting Christians and Christian Churches mainly where Igbos of Southeastern Nigeria worshipped. Boko Haram dispatched suicide bombers and cars loaded with explosives into these places of worship including on Christmas and Easter mass celebration.

Boko Haram has extended further its attacks to gathering spaces of Igbos in the Sabon Gari, Kano. Beer parlors and entertainment centers where Igbos come together for social and entertainment activities were not spared. Transport hub where the Igbos boarded buses transporting their citizens from Kano to Eastern part of the country were also targeted. Thousands have died in these attacks. Boko Haram has also attacked schools in the North, invaded students' dormitories, dragged them out at very early morning hours, and ordered students to identify themselves by their names. Students with names that sounded Christian were singled out, blindfolded and taken away. Students who identified themselves as Christians were eventually beheaded with machetes or execution style on the streets. Jihadists see the students and people attacked as "infidel's representing corrupt Western influence.

Muslim leaders who also criticized or were against the group's ideology and did so publicity have also been targeted and killed. As at December 2013, Boko Haram has increasingly turned its weapons on civilians particularly after locally-formed vigilante groups were out to protect their villages and towns. Some of the villagers acted as mercenaries by providing information to the Joint Military Task Force setup by President Jonathan about the whereabouts and activities of the terrorists. Since Boko Haram acted like gorillas (they attack and fade into the local population), when they wanted. This has posed the greatest challenges to the joint military and police agents going after the terrorists. Their guerilla tactics have been daunting for the security agents that struggle to avoid high civilian casualties as Boko Haram members are known to fade into the population after their attacks.

Boko Haram terrorists have also raided and burnt down several villages whose members of the community refused to accommodate the fighters. The terrorist have sent many residents into the streets as refugees – that is if the villagers made it alive. Sources at the displacement villages disclosed that thousands of villagers had fled and lived on top of hills; they have vacated their homes – if the houses were not razed down; they were taken over and occupied by Boko Haram fighters. The terrorists have not relented in their fight to take over villages in Maiduguri, even with the presence of the international team to assist Nigeria rescue the kidnapped Chibok schoolgirls, the fighters have proved difficult to track and be contained.

Nigeria's federal authorities had initially thought that Boko Haram was an insurgent it could manage on its own without foreign assistance. However, that oversight has been a mistake that the government acknowledged when it finally invited international community for assistance after the Chibok schoolgirls were kidnapped. In retrospect, the British Intelligence reported two weeks before Boko Haram's outright declaration of 'Jihad' in Nigeria in 2009 that an Al-Qaeda-type of group had plans to use Nigeria as a base toward launching attacks on European cities and the United States. The group's threats according to Algerian Secret Service, el-Khabar included using their affiliation with

Al-Qaida to engage in the kidnapping of Westerners across the Sahel region comprising Senegal, Mauritania, Mali, Burkina Faso, Niger, Nigeria, Chad, Ethiopia and Eritrea.[1] From these senseless killing of innocent Nigerians and foreign workers in Nigeria, the group has since showed no restraints even at the time this manuscript was going to press in August 2014. Boko Haram has repeatedly attacked civilians' targets, police, military installations – including the destruction of public and private properties have not stopped. One of its victories in August 2014 was the overrun of a battalion of 500 Nigerian soldiers by Boko Haram fighters. Cameroon Army spokesman, Lt. Col. Didier Badjek said the soldiers had been disarmed and were being accommodated in schools in Cameroon. Boko Haram on Sunday, August 24, 2014 released a video in which it said it had established an Islamic state in the towns and villages it controls in the northeast especially Gwoza. The Nigerian soldiers are in the Cameroonian town of Maroua, about 80km (50 miles) from the Nigerian border, Lt. Col. Badjek told the BBC.[2]

With unending incidents of deadly attacks, it therefore remains to be witnessed how Boko Haram with its affiliations to Al-Qaeda networks in the Middle East, the Mediterranean, and East Africa would ever be dismantled. President Goodluck Jonathan revealed during a conference hosted by French president Francois Hollande in France to address Boko Haram terrorism in Nigeria, and the abduction of 300 Chibok schoolgirls that Boko Haram has killed more than 12,000 Nigerians and foreigners since 2009.[3] Among its victims were mothers, children and fathers. Among them more than 100 passengers killed by a suicide bomber in a parking lot at Sabon Gari, in Kano States known to be a hub of Igbo's from Christian South. The incident occurred a week after the group posted on its website the execution of construction workers it kidnapped with seven other foreigners.

Among foreigners killed were British, Italian, Spanish, and Lebanese. The incident happened simultaneously as Boko Haram used five French family members it kidnapped in border town of Nigeria and Cameroon as bargaining chips for the exchange of Boko Haram members captured by security agents in Nigeria.[4] These events unfolding now, Boko Haram's increasing terror attacks seemed to have been confirmed by the British Intelligence report that came out in 2009, two weeks prior to Boko Haram's outright declaration of 'jihad' to Islamize Nigeria.

WHO ARE BOKO HARAM?

Boko Haram was founded in 2002. It started its military-style operation in 2009 to create an Islamic state in Nigeria. Mohammed Yusuf, who was succeeded by Abubakar Shekau when Yusuf was killed in 2009.Boko Haram has referred to itself as the Nigerian Taliban. It seeks to overthrow the government and replace it with a regime based on Islamic law.[5]

Boko Haram, in Hausa language means, "Western education is sin." The group wants to carve out a separate Islamic state in Nigeria. However, it has targeted schools, as well as Christian churches and police and government offices, in its violent insurgence against the Nigerian state. Boko Haram has not hidden its intentions to transform Nigeria into a Sharia state with its own form of "Taliban" state dominated by the extreme form of sharia laws. The group wants to achieve this goal even if it entails the use of deadly force to accomplish their mission.

Boko Haram has split into various factions. One of the prominent factions is the *Jama'atu Ahlis Sunna Lidda'awati wal-Jihad*, meaning in the same Hausa language "People Committed to the Propagation of the Prophet's Teachings and Jihad." Boko Haram and its splinter groups have three ideological positions, which make understanding each group's real objectives other than violence and taking innocent lives more difficult to comprehend. Boko Haram has commit violence under the common goal of imposing extreme sharia on Nigeria. While one group Boko Haram identifies with the Islamic brotherhood of Al-Qaeda and is inspired by Al-Qaeda transnational goals, the splinter group, Jama'atu Ahlis Sunna Lidda'awati wal-Jihad endorses the criminal activities that include kidnapping of foreigners and domestic political elites that opposed or challenged the fundamentalists or their ideologies.

Before Boko Haram, Nigeria witnessed its internal security threatened by Muslim extremists led by extremists including clerics. One of the most dreaded of the fundamentalists was the Mohammed Marwa group, also known as Maitatsine. The group leader, Marwa, was at the height of his notoriety during the 1970s and 1980s. He was sent into exile by the Nigerian authorities; he refused to believe Mohammed was the Prophet and instigated riots in the country, which resulted in the deaths of thousands of people. Some analysts view Boko Haram as an extension of the Maitatsine riots. [6]

BOKO HARAM TARGETS

Boko Haram targets include Nigerians – Christians and Muslims, Westerners and other foreigners in Nigeria. Three North Korean doctors serving at a hospital in Nigeria's northern Yobe state were killed early Sunday morning on February 10, 2013. The physicians were assisting at Potiskum General Hospital as part of a government agreement with the North Korean government towards implementing and improving health care in Northern Nigeria. The Sunday predawn slayings came on the heels of another deadly attack against medical workers.

On Friday, February 8, 2012, nine health workers who were administering polio vaccinations were killed in Kano, the biggest city in northern Nigeria. Boko Haram's splinter group , Islamic sect, *Jama'atu Ansarul Muslimina Fi Biladis Sudan* (also known as Ansaru) claimed responsibility for killing two Nigerian soldiers along the Lokoja-Okene road. The soldiers were on their way to Abuja to embark on a peacekeeping mission in Mali when they were ambushed and hacked to death. The same *Ansaru* also claimed responsibility for the kidnapped French national in Katsina when 11 foreign construction workers including Lebanese, British, Filipino and other nationals working at a Bauchi construction site were killed. Besides *Ansaru,* other breakaway factions robbed banks and financial institutions while others carried out killings for a price, no matter the individual or his standing in the society.[7]

The origin of Boko Haram and who is behind their financing remains unsubstantiated. President Jonathan has maintained that Boko Haram is proxies and supporters have infiltrated at all levels of his government. Speaking during an inter-denominational church service to mark the 2012 Armed Forces Remembrance Day, President Goodluck Jonathan remarked that some members of the sect were in the executive, legislative and judiciary arms of his government as well as the armed forces. "Some of them are in the executive arm of government; some of them are in the parliamentary/legislative arm of government while some of them are even in the judiciary.[8]

> "Some are also in the armed forces, the police and other security agencies. Some continue to dip their hands and eat with you and you won't even know the person who will point a gun at you or plant a bomb behind your house," the president alerted the nation. [9]

He disclosed that the situation has made it more difficult to combat the nation's security challenges head on. President Jonathan described the present security situation in the country as worse than the civil war experience, insisting, "This is a particular time when the country has major security challenges. There are explosions every day, people are dying and are being killed daily without any reason."[8]

Meanwhile, President Goodluck Jonathan has described as unfortunate, the alleged involvement and sponsorship of Boko Haram, by serving top politicians allegedly linked to the terrorist group. Dr. Goodluck was saying that all those behind the criminalization and politicization of what started as a religious organization would be made to face the wrath of the law. He spoke as fresh facts emerged that there could be more arrests of top political office holders in the weeks ahead, following what top security operatives described as conclusive evidence and intelligence gathering on the alleged link between the group and key sponsors.[9] No political office holder has been sentenced on account of supporting or financing Boko Haram jihadists. It was not until the kidnapping of the Chibok schoolgirls - with the international military and security experts' presence in Nigeria that some military generals and top politicians were interrogated as evidence of captured materials found at locations used by Boko Haram terrorists were allegedly linked to some political leaders in government.

However, the links of Northern politicians Boko Harm come not as a surprise as alleged connections began to emerge. An example of such links, apart from a senator Ali Ndume who was alleged to be connected to the terrorists was an incident on January 14, 2013. On this day, police arrested the suspected mastermind of the Boko Haram 2011 Christmas day bombing. The next day, the suspect escaped from detention. This incident occurred in broad daylight according to witnesses. The escape occurred as he was still wearing handcuffs. Authorities arrested, detained, suspended, and later dismissed a police commissioner for his alleged role in the escape of the suspect. The police commissioner eventually gained his freedom from custody, and there were no further updates on the case.[12] These unfolding events worried Nigerians who expressed concerns that the government could stop Boko Haram if it is determined to do so.

A Nigerian attorney, who wants to be identified only by his first name, Val said, "I think government knows the sponsors of Boko Haram but there is this belief rightly or wrongly that the initial sponsors are no longer in control and that they have lost control of the monster they created. Nevertheless, it takes political will to dig deeper the political will to push security agents a bit harder. This government doesn't seem to have it in this regard."

While the sponsors of Boko Haram are sketchy, it is alleged that by association, the statements attributed to the Former Head of State and national leader of Congress for Progressive Change (CPC), Maj. Gen. Muhammadu Buhari that if he did not win the election, he would make Nigeria ungovernable for President Goodluck Jonathan. "Buhari had previously been credited with a statement that he would make the country ungovernable if the last presidential election did not favor him" - Senior Special Assistant to the President on Public Affairs, Dr. Doyin Okupe revealed in a press statement following interview Buhari had on the Hausa service of the British Broadcasting Corporation (BBC) on March 31, 2013 where he (Buhari) remarked that "The Federal Government should be blamed for the lingering security challenges in the country."[13] That statement, coupled with Buhari's silence on Boko Haram's military-style assaults, in particular Christian Churches bombing on Christmas and Easter eves by Jihadists made his critics claim Mohammadu Buhari knew more about the group and its activities than earlier speculated. Critics also alleged that Boko Haram has financial support from traditional and religious leaders in the North, the majority of whom have been the group persuading President Jonathan to grant amnesty to the Boko Haram members. General Buhari's suspicion of alleged sponsorship of the group focused not just on him but other Northern leaders.

Former Nigeria's Chief of Army Staff (COAS), Lt.-General Azubuike Ihejirika, disclosed Boko Haram's style of operation posed a serious challenge to security forces. Ihejirika disclosed the affiliation of the sect to Al Qaida in the Islamic Maghreb and Al-Shabaab has added an international dimension to the terrorists' membership, their organizational and military-styled operations. COAS said intelligence gathered about the group established that the Islamist sect declared its intent to Islamize the entire Northern states of Nigeria without regard to the constitution of the country. He noted that any country or community whose citizens had a high level of security awareness had higher chances of defeating terrorists.[14]

Whether it is in Afghanistan, Mali or Somali (Libya, Syria) and now Nigeria, the rise of insurgents such as Boko Haram adds a new perspective to violence trying to destabilize Nigeria and other African countries. As witnessed in Afghanistan, Somali and Mali, when these insurgents succeed in destabilizing the state, they are not just making it easy for their networks to have locations to migrate and occupy, the Jihadists would use the occupied spaces to prepare and launch an attack in new targets - other countries. Thus, they are only posing domestic risks, but also are endangerment to the peace and stability of the global village - particularly Jihadists attacking what they considered as Western values and influences they abhorred. The terrorists have never wavered in their interests to attack countries outside their control in particular, the United States and Europe.

As witnessed from Islamic extremists from countries in Afghanistan and the Middle East, the Jihadists never failed to include the United States and Europe as their targets in every opportunity they have used on the Internet or YouTube to relay their messages of hate. It also beats the imagination in Nigeria that few of the terrorists' attacks have been stopped due to intelligence gathering. Most of Boko Haram attacks in Nigeria were sporadic and often surprised authorities as they were to citizens, even when the insurgents issued warnings of their attacks ahead of time. Critics highlight that there were several warnings available that authorities should be able to dictate through intelligence where and if possible when terrorists could attack. It is no wonder that sharing information with US and other international intelligence is very important decision by President Jonathan's government. Experts agreed that the US, British, French, Canadian, and Israeli military and intelligence collaborators have the expertise and the experience to rescue the kidnapped Chibok schoolgirls, and tackle the problems posed by terrorists in West Africa.

Critics of Nigeria's government handling of Boko Haram's terrorism revealed that for the third time, on February 7, 2012, June 25, 2012 and March 14, 2013, the chief of the U.S. Africa Command, Army General Carter Ham warned of threats from Islamic extremists in Africa.[15] Gen. Ham told members of the House Armed Services Committee that if the threats posed by Boko Haram were not curtailed, the risks would increase, and if unchecked, could eventually pose a greater danger to the interests of the United States, and her allies. Gen Ham was being questioned by the committee on why it is important for a robust U.S. military involvement in Africa is necessary after more than a decade of war in Iraq and Afghanistan. Speaking about the danger posed to the U.S., not just Africa by terrorists in the region, Al-Qaeda in Mediterranean (AQIM)-linked terrorists are believed to have played a key role in the attack on September 11, 2012 I the U.S. diplomatic mission attack in Benghazi, Libya that killed four Americans, including U.S. Ambassador Chris Stevens." [16]

In Nigeria, Boko Haram continued to target state, religious, and international institutions as its targets. On March 2013, Boko Haram's splinter group *Jama a'tu Ansaru Muslimina Fi Baladis Sudan*, translated as "Vanguards for the protection of Muslims in Black Africa" claimed it killed 7 foreigners, hostages the Jihadist seized on February 7, 2013 from a construction company, Monitoring Services site in Northern Nigeria. Killed were a Briton, an Italian, a Greek and 4 Lebanese workers. The terror group showed screen shots of dead hostages they claimed were all Christians.[17]

While some Northern leaders claimed Boko Haram and its splinter groups were motivated by poverty, the translation of Boko Haram's name, meaning, "Western education is sin" and *Jama a'tu Ansaru Muslimina Fi Baladis Sudan*, translates as Vanguards for the protection of Muslims in Black Africa. The name ironically, has nothing to do with campaign against poverty inflicting Northern youth, the same youth it sends on suicide mission. Boko Haram's name concisely says a lot about what the group stands for. It is no wonder a cross-section of Nigerians were displeased with statements by some Western leaders such as former President Clinton and Human Rights Leader, Rev. Jesse Jackson suggested Boko Haram violence was caused primarily by the inequality in the distribution of wealth and youth unemployment in Northern Nigeria. [18]

Speaking to reporters in support of the decision by President Goodluck Jonathan to offer amnesty to members of Boko Haram, Jesse Jackson remarked the amnesty program (idea that was later discarded) if properly handled would tackle insecurity in Nigeria. However, he disclosed amnesty must involve economic restitution and rebuilding of mosques and churches destroyed by the terrorists.

"You can bargain and resolve the conflict in the North. That is why I believe so much in non-violence. Non-violence does not

mean fear, but courage and thinking, and it means the
ability to figure it out and fight it out."[19]

Nevertheless, considering that the North in Nigeria (Muslims) has produced majority of heads of states in Nigeria, and knowing the culture
of marginalization, tribalism and favoritism in the allocation of resources in Nigeria based on the party in power or the tribe of the leader; it surprises some observers that these same leaders who have ruled
Nigeria and they are from the North are the ones claiming that the uprising Islamic fundamentalists was as a result of 'poverty.' Critics
asked who were in better position to have fought and reduced poverty
than the leaders now complaining that poverty in the North was responsible for Boko Haram terrorism. "Anyway you look at the situation or the claims by these former leaders who claimed that insurgence
is caused by poverty, it does not make sense," one anonymous critic
remarked.

In hindsight, the marginalization of the South in Nigeria where
the oil wealth of Nigeria is generated has been the root causes of political in fights between the South and North; with the South (mainly
Christians) claiming that wealth from the South is the life support of
Nigeria's economy. More so, there is the perception that the oil wealth
is siphoned and used in developing the North to the disadvantage or
complete neglect of the Southern States in Nigeria. This is at the same
time that some critics also believed the revenue allocation to states
whether North or South is not based on equity rather on population data that is an approximation and "deliberately" favored the North. The
population data also used in the allocation of oil revenue is also said to
be flawed as politicians from South claim that the real population of

Northern States is based on projections and land mass and the data are unrealistic.

Since Northern Nigeria has produced more leaders from the North than South (the North have produced 13 head of states in Nigeria compared to four from the South since Nigeria's independence in 1960); it is based on this political advantage that critics expressed the States in the North should not have more disfranchised youth compared to States in the South. Critics claimed that it beats anybody's imagination, in particular any witness of Nigeria's history who has followed the politics of dichotomy and oil wealth distribution in Nigeria to think that the North that ruled Nigeria that long could claim victims when the reverse should be the case. Majority of Nigerians with access and ownership of auctioned oil wells in Nigeria are from the North. This is also worrisome when the North claims larger population than South, the statistics that the revenue allocation is allocated, and benefits Northern States more compared to South.

The argument is that same Northern elders and politicians who have been in control of national wealth complaining of youth marginalization of "their" Muslim population, then means they are passing judgment about their leadership record that never addressed the problems of the youth in the country (not just North – Muslims or South-Christians). A critic and a concerned Nigerian asked, "Who is therefore responsible for the poverty they are talking about that caused the youths to become terrorists?" "Northern (Muslim) youth's unemployment is not the reason why Boko Haram's terrorists are killing Christians, and Muslims that are against their jihadists' ideology and kidnapping school girls," he expressed.

The States in the North (Muslims) have produced dispropor

tionately more presidents in Nigeria than States in the South. About 13 head of states in Nigeria's 54 years after independence, only four – the late Aguiyi Ironsi, Ernest Oladeinde Shonekan, President Olusegun Obasanjo and President Goodluck Jonathan were Southerners and Christians.[20] General Yakubu Gowon was an only non-Muslim from northern Nigeria. He came from the middle belt, which some Northern political elites still don't consider as Muslim North rather middle belt because of its mixed Christians and Muslims population.

In essence, pundits disclosed that claim that the Northern youth are marginalized is not supported by any concrete evidence, as many Nigerians and observers of Nigeria's history also agreed that like the North, Southern youth have been marginalized by corrupt leaders that cared less about the people but about their pockets and cronies. In Nigeria where the South – Christians have accused the North of disenfranchising the South of oil wealth and using the foreign exchange earned from wealth of Nigeria coming from the South to develop Northern Nigeria (at the expense of Southern States), it means that the Northern youth have not benefitted from North leadership when they have and still occupy key positions at Federal government. It is at the federal government level that the allocation of huge revenue from oil to states every month for infrastructure development, salaries, jobs and other programs. These allocations are based on land mass and population – which the North has advantage over the Southern and Western States in Nigeria

A reflection on the internal politics and dynamics of oil revenue and distribution in Nigeria; an examination of the Nigeria landscape where upon all the wealth a country like Nigeria is endowed, about 60 percent of the population are in abject poverty - it indicates that poverty runs across the country whether North or South. That poverty seems more pronounced in the North is because of poor investment in education and entrepreneurship unlike the south. The evidence that such wealth is not benefiting youth in the North tells a lot about the characters of leaders that have ruled the people. Regrettably, some of the argument made by some of the Western leaders that the unemployment and marginalization of youth from the North is partly responsible for terrorism (re-echoing the opinions of Northern elders and politicians) are not convincing to a majority of Nigerians who wants to see an end to the shedding of precious blood of innocent people by terrorists.

Pundits also warned neither should anybody be persuaded by the argument that the reasons why Boko Haram has killed more than 12,000 people and it is still unrelenting in their assaults including the kidnapping of 300 Chibok school girls whose whereabouts is still unknown is because of poverty. In June, another set of 20 girls were kidnapped very close to Chibok Government Secondary school where the 300 school girls were previously kidnapped.[21] In August 15, 2014, Boko Haram kidnapped a group of young men in Doron Baga, a sandy fishing village in Borno state near the shores of Lake Chad.[22] This time, it took the Chadian Army to free about 75 of the boys while 25 of them are still held captive by their (Boko Haram) abductors.

Similarly, Boko Haram dispatched a female suicide bomber to an army barrack in Nigeria's northeastern city of Gombe on Sunday, June 8, 2014; the bomber's vest exploded killing a soldier, and a guard at the entrance of the military facility. The soldier was searching the vest of the suspect when explosives concealed under her hijab explod ed killing the guard. This happened as eyewitness reported over 110 death-counts in about a week from a string of earlier militant attacks in the area.[23] The reality from increasing frequency of these attacks [in spite of the presence of international military and intelligence experts to assist in the rescue of Chibok schoolgirls] is Boko Haram is undeterred in escalating its campaign to impose strict Islamic laws on largely Muslim Northern Nigeria. While evidence showed that poverty exists in Nigeria that causes violence or brings out violence in some people, the attacks on public property and lives by suicide bombers has nothing to do with poverty. Unfortunately, majority of their victims were poor and innocent Nigerians; the same could be said of young men and women terrorists sent out on suicide missions.

As the chief of the U.S. Africa Command, Gen. Carter Ham appealed, Nigeria needed international support to address the security problems spiraling out of control. General Ham made these pleas in more than three public events in the United States, before the congress and while speaking overseas including in Africa. His pleas was fulfilled when US. Britain, Canada, China, Israel (with Nigeria eventually accepting the assistance) sent technical and intelligence experts to assist Nigeria in the search and rescue of kidnapped Chibok school girls. It often takes a very long time for results to begin to emerge from this kind of rescue mission especially with the number of abducted victims.

The fears emerging after almost 4 months (still counting) of captivity, is that some of the kidnapped Chibok girls may have been assaulted, raped and some killed; others sent against the will on suicide mission. The fears began to emerge as the number of females, 12 -16 year old suicide bombers in month of July through early August 2014 reached an unprecedented level in the history of BokoHaram's deadly attacks on civilians and military personnel. The suspicion was that some of the abducted young girls who refused to change their religion or refused to be raped might have been killed in this manner. It was also gathered accomplice, who stood by, often accompanied these young suicide bombers and use remote control to detonate the improvised explosives strapped on these young girls sent on suicide mission. However, the pledge by President Jonathan to rescue all the girls alive and it was his decision that military force not be used to rescue the girls allows time for Nigeria and international tactical and intelligence team to weigh options that will not jeopardize the lives of the abducted school girls.

Waiting and weighing options are qualities of a good leader. However, there is no doubt Nigeria needs good leadership to build a virile economy, but pursuing these goals in an atmosphere of fear is impossible. President Jonathan has ambition to make Nigeria secured and reach its economic potentials; however, he with one of the brightest team of ministers Nigeria has ever produced may not succeed in an environment of terror and fear. Experts believe that for Nigeria to come out of this situation of insecurity it needs purposeful leadership with support of its people without politics, religion and social dichotomies that are prevailing in the country. Politics in particular has been the weakening link between the people and government causing setbacks and preventing Nigeria leaders from building the type of unity and cohesive team Nigeria needed to accomplish success, not just with its economy, but also eliminate the security risks posed by Boko Haram.

The global community also needs investors rather than donors to make Nigeria reach her full potential. Nigeria cannot afford to be a failed state. Poverty cannot be resolved by food and medical emergency assistances: U.S. or European aid of emergency food rather than help in sustainable development, which Africa needs to achieve lasting poverty reduction.[24]

Lloyd D. Black highlighted the need for U.S. to invest in Africa. Aside from the traditional U.S. humanitarian role, he pointed out that it is in the United States' interest to encourage and accelerate African development along constructive political, economic, and social lines, so African nations may become responsible, and progressive members of the Free World community. He remarked that the U.S. has strategic interests, both military and economic, in a number of African States. With China trade with African countries on the rise, the threat to US interests in Africa has become more threatened than ever before.

With copious human and natural resources - Nigeria like some other countries in Africa cannot be described as country in need of economic assistance. What Africa needs are trade opportunities, tariff-free market zones; quota for export of African products to Europe, Japan, and China. U.S. African agricultural cash crops and minerals are some of the areas of trade negotiations that present concentration on oil export from Nigeria and some oil – rich and gas exporting African nations is denying opportunities to explore these other business sectors. Describing Africa's situation as seen by an expert on Africa trade and business network, "Fish is already abundant; many are willing to catch as many fish as they can." However, government policies and international obstacles on closed doors, tariffs on trade and commerce do obstruct Africa traders (fishermen) from reaching the waters.

While African governments persuade their allies to open their doors to international trade, government must develop its educational system to support present and future development. In May 2011, the government released the findings of the 2010 Nigeria Education Data Survey, a follow-up report to the 2008 NDHS. According to the survey, attendance rates in primary schools ranged from 35 to 80 percent in Nigeria. The lowest attendance rates were in the Northeast and Northwest where rates for boys and girls hovered around 43-47 percent and 35-38 percent, respectively. Overall, 63 percent of boys and 58 percent of girls attended school. According to UNICEF, for every 10 girls in school, more than 22 boys attended school. For young persons between the ages of 17 and 25, about 25 percent had fewer than two years of education. Boko Haram was suspected to have caused the destruction of primary and secondary schools in Bornu and Yobe states.

The attacks in Northeast and Central Nigeria have prohibited an unknown number of children from continuing their education.[25] Meanwhile, with the kidnapping of Chibok School girls and intensified Boko Haram terror attacks, Northern political and religious leaders demanding amnesty for Boko Haram Jihadists have drastically disappeared. President Goodluck Jonathan has rejected the idea even under pressure from Northern political and religious leaders wanting to persuade him along their recommendations to grant amnesty to Boko Haram terrorists. The leaders had claimed that the military response to quell the insurgence was not bringing peace to the region. They also claimed that similar militant group, the Movement for the Emancipation of the Niger Delta (MEND), based in the Southern part of the country that once terrorized Nigerians were granted amnesty in 2009 by the deceased Nigerian President Musa Yar'Adua, a northerner and a

Muslim. They argued that what is good for MEND should also be good for Boko Haram for peace and tranquility to reign.

While the Northern leaders believed that amnesty should be extended to Boko Haram, majority of Nigerians has refused to see any similarity in goals MEND achieved and what Boko Haram is anticipated to achieve. However, it was not in doubt that thousands of MEND militants were granted amnesty by the Federal Government, in spite of the group's wreaked havoc in the oil-rich Niger Delta in southern Nigeria. The reason for irreconcilable differences between Boko Haram and MEND is that MEND was a political-militant group in Niger-Delta region where majority of Nigeria's oil and gas is drilled. MEND's mission was to expose and restrict the exploitation and oppression of the Niger Delta people. MEND also promotes using militant response to protect the Niger-Delta environment from pollution by oil drilling corporations.

MEND perceived the Federal Government neglect of the devastation of the environment as collaboration between oil companies and the Nigeria federal government. They claimed that these corporations maintained high ethical and environment standards in their countries of origin in Europe and the United States, but government has allowed them to degrade the environment and hold nobody or company accountable for deaths and long-term environmental devastation that have everlasting implications on the environment and life in the Niger-Delta area of Nigeria.

MEND also wanted a greater share of the oil revenue for the devastation caused by pollution on the people in the area. Majority of Niger-Delta citizens still live in abject poverty even as Nigeria oil revenue comes from their land with devastating pollution. The Federal government negotiated settlement that included special oil revenue allocation to the state, and negotiation with the oil corporations to protect the environment from future pollution.

Chapter 2.

The Real Financiers of Boko Haram
- Financial Cash Flow and Its Global Terror
Networks

In 1998, there were simultaneous attacks on U.S. embassies in Dar es Salem, Tanzania and Nairobi, Kenya. Ten Kenyans died in the attack and three Israelis, two of them children. Almost as this particular attack was taking place, two shoulder-launched Strela 2 (SA-7) surface-to-air missiles were launched by Al-Qaeda affiliated terrorists at another chartered Boeing 757 airliner owned by Israel-based Arkia Airlines, as it was taking off from Moi International Airport.

Before 9/11, terrorists in Kenya and Tanzania took African lives when U.S. embassies were targets. If it may be recalled, East Kenyan-born Fazul Abdullah Mohammed masterminded the attacks on the two embassies. The attacks brought attention to Bin Laden, who then made the FBI's most wanted list. Al Qaeda undoubtedly carried out the bombing in response to American involvement in the extradition and alleged torture of four Egyptian Islamic Jihad (EIJ) members arrested in Albania two months before the explosion in Kenya and Tanzania took place. As these simultaneous patterns of bombings were the trade mark of Al Qaida, the 1998 bombings of the U.S. Embassies in Nairobi and Dar es Salaam killed 224, including 212 Africans, 12

Americans, and more than 5,000 were injured.[1] In essence, Africans were majority victims in all these attacks, a fact that President Obama reiterated as he addressed youth in his June 2013 meeting with African youth at Soweto in Johannesburg, South Africa. However, with all these attacks, attention to the war on terror has not been focused on Africa but rather on Afghanistan, Iraq and Pakistan, even though there is a strong network of Al-Qaeda, not just in Somalia, but also in West Africa.

Therefore, when on June 2, 2013, the United States posted a $23 million reward for information that would help track down the five leaders of militant groups in West Africa, the U.S. State Department Rewards for Justice program identified the wanted fugitives behind the spreading of terror in the region; the decision marked the first ever bounties posted for wanted militants in West Africa. It was welcome as a turning point from the Africa's front on the war on terror since 9/11 even though pundits disclosed that it came too late.

The highest reward of $7 million was offered for the Boko Haram leader, Abubukar Shekau along with another $5 million each for Al-Qaeda veteran Moktar Belmokhar, the one-eye Islamist behind the Algerian gas plant attack in January in which about 37 foreigners including three Americans were killed, and AQIM leader, Yahya Abou Al-Hamam, involved in the murder of elderly French hostage in Nigeria. This evidence showed not just the global outreach of Boko Haram, but that its financial network has become a source of serious concern to Nigeria and the United States security departments. A week before the United States placed the bounties on the suspected terrorists; Boko Haram called on the Islamists in Afghanistan, Pakistan, and Iraq to join the bloody fight to create an Islamic state in Nigeria.[2] The same outreach call was made by Boko Haram leaders to Al-Qaeda in the Islamic Maghreb, Afghanistan, and Pakistan when in May the Federal Government sent troops to combat the terror. The terror group also made a similar call for support from Al-Qaeda around the world when it was overwhelmed by both air and land attacks on the terror group in May 2013.

These liaisons notwithstanding, an examination of the Boko Haram ideologies as posted on its website showed a domestic terror group based in Northern villages in Borno State, Nigeria. It is founded on the same philosophy of using terror to achieve its goal to Islamize Nigeria, and at the same time destabilize the country, while using it as a base to reach its targets in the West, particularly the United Kingdom and the United States. In its mission statement, Boko Haram declared itself as the Congregation and people committed to the propagations of the Prophet's teachings and jihad in the Nigeria Sharia conflict. It has as its ideology – Islamic extremism, Islamic Fundamentalism – *Tafir*; its area of operations Northern Nigeria, Northern Cameroon, Niger and Chad, its allies; Al-Qaeda in the Islamic Maghreb; its opponents – Nigeria State. Battle – included the Nigeria Sharia Conflict and 2009 Nigeria sectarian violence. These words were in verbatim what exactly Boko Haram stated it stood for, and more, since the kidnapping and killings of Westerners, is also part of its mission. The fact that its name translates to "Western Education is sacrilegious" was not included in its motto shows a terror group whose agenda has increased and is not in any way relenting in its blood bath on innocent citizens by using sophisticated commandos, and military–style weapons and suicide bombers to achieve its goals.

As witnessed with its objectives and international networks, the connection to these networks has also been the same motivation for its funds. In essence, the several links to these international terror organizations have extended Boko Haram's financial outreach. Initially, it started with individual members' contributions. Those contributions started in 1995, when the terror group operated under the name Shabaab – a Muslim youth organization. At that period, Mallam Lawal was its leader. When Lawal left the youth organization to further his education, the group, under its new leader, Mohammed Yusuf, turned into a political organization. Under Yusuf, the group also received donations from notable Muslims in the North. One particular prominent donor donated a bus and loud speakers to the organization. Mohammed Yusuf's father –in-law, Baba Fugu, donated a farm at Auno village in Konduga, a Local Government Area of Borno State. The farm was later converted to the group's first training camp.[3]

Among Boko Haram's major sponsors was a "businessman" from Bauchi State in Nigeria who has a link with Al-Qaeda in Somalia. He was alleged to have received training from Abu Umar Al-Wadud, the leader of Al-Qaeda in Somalia. It was gathered the businessman escaped Nigeria in 2009 following the attack by security agencies in Nigeria to flush out Boko Haram leaders and dislodge the group. Thus, he was forced him to relocate to Somalia.

On national territory, when Nigeria was returning to democratic rule in 1999, and the political campaign was on a new start, some local politicians were supporting extreme Islamic manifestos and policies in the North states of Nigeria. Some gubernatorial candidates were openly contesting on the ground that they will Islamize Northern Nigeria if elected into office. At the time, the terror group was evolving also. In fact, the campaign to introduce Sharia across Northern States came to fruition when in October 22, 1999, Sanni Ahmed Yerima, and then elected Governor of Zamfara State made the initial announcement on its introduction of Sharia in the state. He followed his promise to the citizens and presented a Sharia bill that passed into law in Zamfara in January 2000. Governor Yerima's determination to further Islamic laws across the North was not hidden. Between 1999 and 2000, he led 14 other Northern states in Northern Nigeria to adopt Sharia laws in their states.

Meanwhile, some politicians found a common ground not only to associate with the group, which in 2001 adopted the name Boko Haram. Boko Haram under the leadership of Mohammed Yusuf opened the group to political influence and popularity in 2002. This was as political campaigns were going on, hoping to win elections for political party of interest, but also with the bigger agenda of introducing a sharia state in Borno State. As revealed by Yusuf when the group was launched in Maiduguri, Boko Haram's goal was always to establish a sharia state in Bornu State. With financial support from Ali Modu Sheriff, who later became the Governor of Bornu State, the groups expanded its powers. A testimony that Boko Haram's emergence and funding have political undertones came with the statement by Boko Haram's member arrested on November 3, 2011 by the operatives of State Security Service. In a piece by Associate editor of the *Nation* Taiwo Ogundipe, the Boko Haram member identified as Ali Sanda Umar Konduga alias Usman al-Zawahiri (named after the leader of Al-Qaeda after the death of Osama Bin Laden) unraveled the riddle about the funding of the Boko Haram.

According to testimony through an interpreter by Konduga, Mohammed Yusuf, Boko Haram's late leader, who was killed in police custody in 2009, trained him. He also revealed that Boko Haram had origins in a militia group known as ECOMOG. The name is an adaptation of the military arm of the Economic Community of West African States (ECOMOG) known for its military interventions to bring peace in the West African region. Boko Haram's ECOMOG was a political youth militant group formed in 2003. The ECOMOG is said to have provided Boko Haram more members and military training. The Presidential Committee on Security Challenges in the North-East Nigeria, chaired by Ambassador Usman Galtimari, has disclosed that ECOMOG created the fertile ground for the speedy growth and the spread of Boko Haram.[4]

Boko Haram member identified as Ali Sanda Umar Konduga claimed that an ex-Governor Sheriff was the financier of the group at a point. He disclosed that an ex-Governor Sheriff even appointed their leader, Fugi Foi, as a commissioner in the state. "When Foi was sacked and then killed, the sect believed that his death was political and swore to avenge it." He disclosed that it was then that the late Saidu Pindar, Nigeria Former Ambassador to Sao Tome and Principle stepped in as a major financier of the sect and promised them N10 million. Konduga, alias Al-Zawari, revealed that Pintar was on his way to deliver N5 million to Boko Haram when he had a motor accident and died.[5]

Pintar died on August 31, 2011 along Kaduna –Zaria road. Before his death, he sought election under People Democratic Party (PDP) as a running mate to the gubernatorial candidate, Mohamadu Goni. Konduga revealed that it was Pintar that nicknamed him Al-Zawahiri to conceal his (Konduga) identity for security reasons.[6] Konduga also said that a surviving Senator in the Federal Republic of Nigeria, Mohammed Ali Ndume later took over the sponsorship of the sect after Pintar's death.[7] Ndume was a two-term member of the House of Representatives on the platform of All Nigeria People's Party (ANPP). He also served as a Minority Leader of his party in the House of Representative before he joined the People' Democratic Party (PDP) in 2011 in order to contest for the Senate in 2011, which he won. Ndume was arrested by State Security Service (SSS) in Nigeria. He was detained and later released.

Sources of Boko Haram's money are also traced to neighbor state Governors of Kano and Bauchi. According to an unnamed interviewee, a member of the Boko Haram held under detention by the Nigeria State Security Services, the immediate Governor of Kano State , Ibrahim Shekarau had promised in 2004 to an initial monthly payment of $5 million and later raised the monthly payment to N10 million. He disclosed that apart from these monthly payments, the government of Shekarua provided institutional infrastructure support through the Hisbah (Islamic Police) project, which received an annual budgetary allocation of N1.01 billion. All these promises, including the funding of the "Islam Police," were stopped when a new Governor of the State, Rabiu Kwankwaso took over power in Kano State.[8]

In Bauchi State, the detainee also revealed that an agreement was reached with the incumbent Governor Isa Yuguda in 2008 for a monthly payment of N10 million. The agreement, the source disclosed, included the provision of training grounds on the mountains scattered in Bauchi State, in addition to guaranteed protection against, arrest by the Federal Government. The detainee said that the Bauchi State Governor stopped the monthly funding in mid-2011, but the group was not mad because of the access the state offered the members to use the mountain tops located in the state for training. However, he remarked that since the group was not happy with the development involving the stoppage of their monthly payments and *Hisbah,* Islamic Police project, the group still decided to wage massive assaults on Kano Metropolis and Bauchi city leading to the deaths of hundreds of people.

While the two state governments mentioned denied their involvement, Boko Haram's spokesperson remarked, "Northern Governors are overwhelmed about the strength of the group and are aware of the capabilities of Boko Haram operatives in the prospective states." Some of the state government officials the interviewee disclosed "visit their camps to watch them in training exercises. The training is harder than that of the Nigerian military."[9] All Nigeria Peoples Party (NPP) former Deputy Chairman, and a retired General in the Nigeria Armed Forces, Brigadier Genial Jeremiah Useni (rtd.), while on a visit to Borno State, witnessed many young people selling petroleum products in the open streets, and he asked the Governor why the young people were allowed to engage in illegal trading in petroleum products; the Governor's response was "…leave them, they are useful to us (during general elections as thugs), we use them to turn everywhere meaning to stir trouble."[10]

As the book was about to go to press, the military Joint Task Force, detained the chairman of the All Nigeria Peoples Party (ANPP in Borno State), Mala Othman over the suspicion that he has links with the *Jamaá Ahl a-sunnah lida'wa wa al-jihad*, better known by its Hausa name as Boko Haram. Othman's arrest followed the July 2013 attack of 30 students of Federal Government College.[11] Potiskum town, Yobe state was invaded in the early morning hours with many slaughtered by gunmen suspected to be Boko Haram. Othman's house was also set ablaze by the Youth Volunteers group christened "Civilian

JTF" but who are identified as vigilante youths against Boko Haram.

Since Boko Haram is considered a major political threat to Nigeria, Africa Command (AFRICOM) Commander, General Carter F. Ham confirmed in September 2011 that the terror group with other African and global terror groups are targeting Westerners and specifically, the U.S.; he said that their synchronization of their efforts entailed raising funds across international boundaries to achieve their goals. While Boko Haram's funding is local, it seemingly enjoyed the same international support from the United Kingdom and Saudi Arabia. Replacing the Afghanistan' situation in Nigeria entailed funding floating across the world including some Islamic organizations such as Al Muntada Trust Fund with headquarters in the United Kingdom and the Islamic World Society with headquarters in Saudi Arabia. [12] Other sources of funding of Boko Haram is linked to the global and transnational criminal activities that include kidnapping for ransom, drug trafficking, weapons trafficking and armed robbery. [13]

The former chief of Nigeria Army Staff (COAS) Lt General Azubuike Ihejirika told reporters in an interview that the Army did recognize the involvement of foreigners in the operation of Boko Haram. He said that the weapons and other sophisticated military ammunitions captured from the group did establish foreign backers to the group. He said these are strong evidence of foreign involvement in the terrors taking place in Nigeria. "The types of weapons we have captured, the type of communication equipment and the expertise Boko Haram has displayed in the preparation of improvised explosives devices...these are pointers to the fact that there is international involvement in the terrorism going on in Nigeria."[13]

When then Senator Ali Modu Sheriff built a mosque and established an Islamic school, he opened the doors to the school to poor families from across Nigeria and neighboring Niger and Chad – two countries with open borders to Nigeria. The goal of sending these children to the Islamic Center was to train them in extreme Islamic (sharia) principles. However, the objective quickly shifted to use the center for training of future jihadists to fight the state of Nigeria. As such, schools have been known to exist in Afghanistan and Iraq, their financial outreach and assistance from Islamic organizations and institutions around the world are in no doubt.

For the Boko Haram national and international agenda, members of the terrorist group apprehended by Federal Authorities in Nigeria revealed that the group depended on donations by members, fundamentalists politicians including Governors and Senators in the Northern States, Boko Haram's link with Al-Qaeda in the Islamic Maghreb (AQIM) and Al-Qaeda in the Middle East has added more to the channels of funding for the group with far outreach to other Islamic organizations in United Kingdom and Saudi Arabia. [14]

While Boko Haram continued to wreck damages and costs to human lives and property, the attempt by the Federal government to dislodge, and probably eliminate the terror network has gradually started yielding results as the Joint Task Force including all the arms of Nigeria Armed Forces has put the terror group on the run. While the group has dispersed, it continues to engage in sporadic killings using Motor bicycles and means such as open confrontation with the Joint Military Task Force comprising the State Secret Service (SSS), the military and police. These attacks were in spite of the Federal Government's state of emergency in Nassarawa, Borno and other neighboring states.

However, with all the efforts the authorities in Nigeria are making to dislodge Boko Haram, the group's financial links in Nigeria and overseas are yet to be addressed. The intention by the Federal Government to introduce Paperless Money Transactions in key states in Nigeria is part of the efforts to control of flow of cash to the terror groups. Nevertheless, as pundits have disclosed, most of the financial transactions by terror groups are by cash, through either the black market or underground economic transactions. Because of a lack of efforts on the Federal Government of Nigeria to stop money laundering including money going to Boko Haram and other terrorist organizations in Africa and Middle East, Nigeria was threatened to be blacklisted by the international anti-monetary laundering watchdogs over Nigeria's inability to track the source of funds of the dreaded Islamic group, the Boko Haram.

The Financial Action Task Force (FAFT), an organization renowned for setting the global standards for measures to combat money laundering, terrorist and proliferation financing disclosed that Nigeria is not cooperating despite early warnings for the country to comply with the rules. In its report in May 2012, FAFT listed Nigeria among the countries that have not made any significant progress in addressing the huge problems identified by Anti-Money Laundering and Combating Terrorism Financing (AML/CTF) regimes.[15]

Chapter 3

Boko Haram – Exploiting the Art of Media Publicity & Propaganda

Like Al-Qaeda in the Middle East and the Al-Shabaab in the Mediterranean, Boko Haram enjoys and thrives in publicity. With the international media focusing attention on the group, Boko Haram utilizes the opportunity to the full and even goes the extra length to feed the media with You-Tube videos as part of its propaganda effort. Unfortunately, Boko Haram has often received more attention individuals and their family members who were killed or maimed by the suicide bombs by the terror group. The media publicity also gives the Jihadists an opportunity to recruit followers.

There is no doubt that individuals hurt by Jihadists' assaults and their families deserved more attention in media than the extremists receive from the same media. As evidence showed including the timeline of Boko Haram attacks that the terrorists were more often in the news for the wrong reasons. Not only are these jihadists in the headline news, they also continue their bombing and blood-bath mayhem even as the Federal Government Nigeria sets up an amnesty committee at the cabinet level of government to consider whether to negotiate an amnesty with the group, and under what conditions for purposes that include avoiding more bloodshed. Northern elders (religious and political), along with some Southern politicians have mounted pressure on

President Jonathan to look into the option of granting members of Boko Haram amnesty. Supporters of the amnesty initiative believed it would reduce deaths and security threats that the group posed to the national security of Nigeria.

However, as the negotiations for the amnesty was on the way, Boko Haram leaders continued their attacks on civilians, police, military and government agencies that they considered a threat to the goals of the organization. Boko Haram has also issued threats to media organization that do not give them publicity. The terror group considered any media that does not report the activities of the terror group "objectively" as its enemy despite the disastrous bloodbath and deaths on the streets in the North that media highlights. In essence, Boko Haram is conveying the message that in spite of the bloodbath unleashed on Nigerians, and the security threat the group poses to the stability of Nigeria, its leaders are not satisfied that the media was paying more attention to the deaths and not what causes those carrying arms to attack innocent citizens.

In the mindset of terrorists, the media that attempted to report the truth and feed the federal government information about Boko Haram has been warned by the group's leader Shakur of disastrous consequences "if the media doing so does not report accurately." Shakur went further to cite the experience of *This Day* newspaper in 2002 when pre-Miss World fundamentalists rioted and razed the newspaper Miss Isioma Daniel's report that allegedly blasphemed Prophet Mohammed. Shakur warned those newspapers that do not report "accurately" about Boko Haram will face the same consequences, meaning that the newspaper will be burnt down, and the journalist killed. Daniel, a young columnist, fled to Norway when fundamentalists declared

Fatwa on her head following her satirical article on *This Day* newspaper that queried the rioting against the Miss World pageant in Nigeria.

The fundamentalists have opposed the pageant as Western culture that disrespects women and show women nudity, which is against sharia laws. Daniel published that the rioters should stop and hypothesized that Mohammed would have loved Miss World taking place, even perhaps taking one of the contestants as his wives. The rioters killed 200 Nigerians and forced the Miss World pageant cancelled, and held in Alexandria Hall in the heart of London instead of Abuja, the original venue of the contest. The preliminary sessions of the pageant had concluded and the finals were taking place when the rioters struck Abuja.

Boko Haram contradictory philosophy and its action are part of a ploy by the group to gain media attention. For example, in January 2012, Abubakar Shekau claimed that the group was carrying out attacks on Christians in retaliation for the killing of Muslims by Christians in central Nigeria, including Kaduna and Plateau states. Boko Haram leader 'Imam Abubakar Shekau' sent a message to the president through YouTube Message to President Jonathan.[1] Similarly, in December 2010, following attacks on Christmas Eve 2010 in the cities of Jos and Maiduguri, Boko Haram released a statement claiming the attacks were to avenge "atrocities committed against Muslims.[2] Once, Boko Haram "disparaged" and "disliked" Western technology, but now found it useful in their violent attacks on civilian targets. In practice, cellular phones, automobiles, video cameras, You-Tube and the Internet have been effective in their propaganda to win members and propagate their ideologies, which, unfortunately, the media is indirectly assisting the group by the frequency of publicity they receive. Boko

Haram's use of modern technology and the mediated media to get their messages across has been unfortunately successful in getting their messages of blood assaults and terror on the population.

Since 2009 when they commenced suicide bombing and kidnapping, Boko Haram has not conceded in using the media to inform authorities either before or after they carried out attacks including the Easter Sunday attack of a Catholic Church in the city of Kaduna where more than 36 people were killed by a suicide bomber riding in a bomb-loaded vehicle.[3] Boko Haram has unleashed a 42-month multi-pronged attack on military, police and security facilities, and churches that claimed more than 3000 lives. [4] And on most of these attacks; however, they have claimed responsibility using the media to publicize their acts. The group has also killed and kidnapped some Westerners as hostages. With the French and Malian troops engagement in Northern Sudan (which successfully led to the flushing of the jihadists out of Mali and the flight of their descendants into the desert while others infiltrated the general public and neighboring states), the danger the jihadists pose to Nigeria and other African countries' internal security cannot be underestimated.

The ammunitions at the disposal of the Jihadists were found to be more sophisticated military weapons than the military has in its arsenal. Some of them traceable to the fall of Libya and the looting of ammunition depots by the public. The lack of attention to protect the arms getting into the wrong hands such as Al-Qaida and other radical groups was what pundits claim the media missed.

The media was occupied with the overthrow of Gadhafi and not with the security of Libya, the region, and Africa. The media is repeating the same pattern of reporting by not addressing where the insurgents – the jihadists had fled with their weapons, rather the media is paying too much attention to the French presence in Mali and the historical implications of past experiences of Mali and the France's relationship post colonization and whether the French are staying or leaving Mali soon.

The situation explains why pundits are calling for a new part for the international media) in reporting Africa in the 21st century. The old form of reporting by the media to appeal to a local audience in an era of Information Communication technology (ICT), and with mediated media, need a paradigm shift in ways international media report Africa.

- *BOKO HARAM AND THE CONSPIRACY THEORISTS*

Nigeria is an oxymoron. It is a country endowed with abundantly human and material resources yet seems to reinvent the wheel of progress and turn those abundant human and material resources into wealth that will help its own people. With the Boko Haram's terror attacks, there is a rise and spread of those conspiracy theories among Nigerians. Even though some conspiracies have floated that alleges that Northern Nigeria – mostly Muslims were milking Nigeria oil to develop the North – mostly Christians to the detriment of the South, conspiracy theorist believed that the North is involved in this tactics so that they could finally declare their own Islamic country governed by sharia laws.   Similarly, the prediction by some Western pundits that Nigeria will be a failed state in 2015 add more suspicion to the causes of some tensions including Boko Haram that threaten the internal security of Nigeria. Boko Haram has gone the length in ensuring that Nigeria is a failed state. According to several statements attributed to Boko Haram members and obtained from eye witnesses including those by Human Rights Watch in 2012, the terror group no doubt is striking at Christians for many reasons. Boko Haram claims that they attack "Christians to avenge the atrocities committed against Muslims," undermine "disbelievers and their allies and all those who support them," [5] and "liberate ourselves and our religion from the hands of infidels and the Nigerian government" as part of a "full scale war between the Muslims and the Christians."[6]

Boko Haram violence against Christians has included the torching and blowing up of churches, and carrying out abductions, forced conversions, and attacks in markets and during religious services using guns, improvised explosive devices, or suicide bombers. During the July 2009 violence, for example, witnesses in Maiduguri said that Boko Haram fighters torched churches, killing men hiding inside the holy place. They also abducted Christians and took them to Yusuf's compound. Boko Haram members also killed Christian men after they refused to convert to Islam.[7]

Boko Haram's attacks on Christians has resulted in deaths, and forced conversion of Christians to Islam. They have also sparked sectarian clashes in already volatile states. On three successive Sundays in June 2012, for example, suicide bombers detonated explosives at church services in Bauchi, Bauchi State; Jos, Plateau State; and Zaria and Kaduna, Kaduna State—all locations of past episodes of intercommunal violence.[8] The attacks on two churches in Zaria and a church in Kaduna killed at least 21 people and set off several days of reprisal and counter-reprisal killings. The clash between Christians and Muslims resulted in 80 more deaths.[9]

Similarly, the Christmas Eve 2010 bomb blasts in Christian communities in Jos sparked a month of sectarian bloodletting that claimed around 200 Muslim and Christian lives.[10]

Amidst staggering corruption and mismanagement of resources by political leaders, a cross section of Nigerians believe that politicians "fabricate" some of these conspiracy theories to distract the masses while they loot the system. For Boko Haram, there is the Conspiracy of the West to Rule the World by destroying Islam: First, there is no doubt conspiracy theories are not particular to Nigeria. There are individuals worldwide who believe in one conspiracy or the other. Either they believe, for example, that 6 out of the 19 hijackers that flew jets into the World Trade Center in the U.S. are alive or they believe that it was not terrorists, but "others" who did it. Others believe that the 911 attack was the U.S. government's conspiracy to go to war and occupy Iraq and maintain their presence in Middle East or/and for the sake of oil.

Similarly, some believe that the idea of Apollo Moon landing was a real or a hoax. But for humans, as long as they exist, there are bound to be ordinary men and women, who are fairly or unfairly motivated to believe what they want to. However, it becomes troubling when such unfounded and unsubstantiated beliefs are made real, and used for the recruitment of future terrorists in Nigeria or elsewhere.

However, it should not be taken for granted that political elites and clerics frame these conspiracy theories in their efforts to persuade and win converts to their side. For instance, in Nigeria where Boko Haram has gained ground, the teaching of clerics that see others not holding their religious views as "infidels" and must be converted or destroyed seem to be working especially since there are no institutions established either by the state or Christian religious organizations and institutions to counter these erroneous "religious ideologies."

In Northern Nigeria, some religious organizations use videos that are ant-West to teach their pupils. Some of these religious clerics and politicians sometimes go the length of distributing the anti-West videos to Christians either for reason that may include seeking new converts or as their own personal or groups' campaign to show the West that Southerners in Nigeria welcome are, but "traitors." In all circumstance, the goal of clerics spreading these propaganda materials and conspiracy theories have their goal of reaching out to the youth whose mind are still not developed, but have the trust reposed by the parents of the youth that the clerics are teaching their children to be upright Muslims. As evidence from suspected and convicted terrorist arrested in either Britain or the United States have shown, these were youths indoctrinated by their mullahs to commit crimes that the young people may not be willing to do or carry out on their own.

In all levels of the fundamentalists' indoctrination of young people, it has been a gradual persuasive process that aims to radicalize the youth. In some circumstances, the youth were self-radicalized by their peers whose goals are to destroy innocent lives because lessons they were taught is that their religion is under attack by "Powers" that want to rule the world by destroying values and people or religion they hold very strongly dear. The effort to put the "powers" that want their religion extinct on defense will improve the chances of their survival. In essence, the fight to resist the influence of these "Powers" and the survival for their religion and culture that is under attack entails the defense of it, even if it means the death of innocent people and the suicide bomber.

Regrettably, there is no particular place that this mentality of using conspiracy theory as a recruitment tool more than in "religious" schools" in Nigeria where countries in the Middle East and Muslim-populated countries in Asia support and fund these schools. In Nigeria, the recruitment of would- be terrorists goes on subtly underground. It is not only the clerics that use the tactics of propagating conspiracy theories to recruit new Muslim converts and would-be terrorists but politicians. The irony is that some these educated extremists have their children schooling in Europe and the United States. They also live Western life-styles including living in expensive homes. They use the rhetoric and sometimes the videos of conspiracies such as "The West and Double-Speak" and the Illuminati theories to deceive, brainwash, and motivate the unemployed youths to take arms in the name of jihad against the infidels.

In Nigeria, like the rest of the world, there are a majority of peace-loving Muslims. However, like anything that is destructive and gains easy attention, the bad tends to dominate. However, for the majority to show that they are in control of defending the name and image of Islam, they must not allow the few to be dictating and directing the discourse about a peaceful religion. To show tolerance of other religions and those that practice those other religion, they must show that they are part of the solution to the terrorists and their destruction of the lives of "infidels." They must intervene when these videos and rhetoric against other religion are being played and circulated by the clerics and some Muslims that appear to be moderate, yet clandestinely propagate hate and destruction because their religion is under attack. They must ensure that fund-raising and infiltration of money into schools that teach extreme religious faith do not exist in their communities.

In Nigeria, not only do these schools exist, but also they have supporters. In the media, some that believe in the conspiracy theories have access to writing expressing their opinions. For example in the month of May 2013, when Boko Haram has already killed more than 3,600 Nigerians and foreigners (Europeans, Americans, Asians, and Lebanese); two British (of Nigerian parents), Michael Adebowale, 22, and Michael Olumide Adebolajo, 28, attacked, 25-year-old British soldier Lee Rigby with knives and a meat cleaver on the open street outside the Woolwich army barracks in southeast London. Rigby was stabbed to death, Nigerian writer, Femi Kani–Kayode remarked: "Was this whole thing (referring Woolwich incident) to some kind of state-sponsored ¬ Illuminati-style human sacrifice? Was it designed and orchestrated by the authorities to create more terror in the land and to give them the opportunity to introduce more draconian laws, curb immigration and do away with even more civil liberties on the grounds that they wish to fight the very terror that they themselves created?" 11 Fani- Kayode, a Christian, asked readers, if anyone doubts his assertion that they ought to do themselves a favor and watch David Icke's revealing documentary titled "9/11- *It was an Inside Job*". It is on YouTube, he said. He also urged readers to find Icke's many books and watch his various. Their worldview will change dramatically after watching these, he disclosed.

He said it is important to note the two suspects were not just British citizens of Nigerian descent, but were both Muslim converts. He remarked that is to say they were both brought up as Christians, and then somewhere along the line, they converted not just to Islam but to its most extreme and radical brand of Islam. Fani-Kayode asked, who cultivated them, and took them to this point, and how did it get so bad?

He claimed that the whole episode is a ritual murder' which provides the western powers and the British people another reason to demonize Islam and target mosques and Muslim clerics. Yet, he remarked, even if you do not agree with me on anything that I have said here, "the questions that I have raised are legitimate, and they are indeed food for thought"[12]

Fani-Kayode is an attorney. He was in government as a special assistant to the former President of Nigeria, Olusengun Obasanjo before his appointed as Aviation Minister. Therefore, the ethos or credibility of person of his caliber does get to the some people to send the wrong message. Unaware to him, youth wanting to find reasons to join Boko Haram are motivated by this style of rhetoric. Fani-Kayode's article received wide circulation.

Boko Haram, even though its name means "Western education is sinful," ironically, its members do receive all their messages through western –developed technologies; even from their hiding caves in Niger-Nigeria boundary hills and caves where the jihadist now hide following assaults by the Joint Military Task Force to destroy the group. Fani-Kayode comes from the south where he is of Yoruba extract. His religion and tribe make his statement more credible and appealing to some groups and extremists; this is when his comments are compared to similar statements from ordinary Muslim on the street or even Muslim fundamentalists and mullahs. These words of Western

Power's attempts to wipe Islam from the face of the earth are part of extremists recruiting rhetoric.

While some disagree that the premise is far from the truth, there are trending domestic conspiracy theories. Among them is the North using the wealth from the North to develop Northern Nigeria to the disadvantage of the South in anticipation that Nigeria will eventually break apart and the North will escape with wealth derived from South and make Mecca of break-way Northern Nigeria. There is also a conspiracy theory that the Muslim elites and politicians were the financiers and guide to fundamentalists' rage and violence against Christians - Igbos in particular. Boko Haram, the theorists claim was bred and financed by Northern political elites to make Nigeria ungovernable as a statement by former President, Mohamadu Buhari indicated, even though he has dismissed that he meant that. However, many Southerners believed that the terrorism on Nigeria soil was part of the Northern elite's agenda to make Nigeria ungovernable for President Jonathan who happens to be a Christian from the South.

As more Northern Muslims of Fulani descent now migrating into Southern parts of Nigeria in the name of ranchers or "selling cows," there is also a conspiracy theory that follows these nomads around in the Eastern region of the country as they trade their stocks. The conspiracy theory is that Northern politicians and mullahs are dispatching these Fulani cattle ranchers as foot soldiers for bigger agenda. who are known nomads but now using the roving movement and life styles as a disguise for foot soldiers (jihadists) ready to strike at any moment. Incidents of Hausa-Fulani cattle ranchers migrating south attacking villagers in the Southeastern states in Nigeria attacking Igbos (Christians) with machetes and AK 47 riffles have been on the rise. There were also incidents of these nomads mounting illegal check points with the goal of stopping passenger vehicles and robbing passengers. Since these nomads are in every part of Igbo land, they are gradually springing up mosques in the southeastern states of Nigeria, and few Southerners are gradually converting to Islam and preaching their acceptance into the community.

While there has been just one incident of suicide bombing in Lagos in the month of July 2014, there have not been such threats in the south. Threat to peace abound in Jos – middle belt zone of the country where the same Nomads were received and over the years, migration of these "foot soldiers" had progressed with death tolls in thousands of Christians as a result of sectarian violence. Some pundits have warned that the Southern States opening their doors to these Muslim Nomads should be careful before the experiences in Jos and Benue States repeat in the South.

In essence, the theory is that these Nomads are not only selling their merchandise – cows as they travel through every Southern States, but they are like surveyors mapping the routes and location for an eventual jihadists attack that may be on their long term goal of Islamizing the South. Pundits say that it is just a matter of time, while other disagree that these nomads are following their pattern of lifestyle that dated more than a thousand years.

No matter how dismal theorists may be about the movement of Nomads – Muslim jihadists migrating to the South in the disguise of ranchers or "cattle sellers," while Christians are targeted in the North by Book Haram, the Christians in the South are welcoming these Muslim "jihadists" in the south and buying their cows and providing them money   for   their   eventual   war   to   Islamize   Nigeria.

As an observer of Nigeria Muslim and Christian relationships observed, the patronage of the Muslim nomads (cattle sellers) by Christians (Igbos in particular) in the South shows about the dynamic personalities and cultural value of tolerance and acceptance that are inherent in Nigeria culture irrespective of love and hate relationships between Muslim and Christians; relationships that are often determined by politicians and clerics for their personal and selfish political goals.

Since the jihadists' target is majority Igbos of the South eastern and Christians, there is no doubt that the fundamentalist groups have as their priority goal, the Islamization of Nigeria, and they envisage that the Igbos are the strongest in terms of numbers (population that are not Muslims yet), will power, and economic power. Therefore, weakening these powers will be an easy road to conquering them and other groups in Nigeria. On another view, Boko Haram's perception of Igbos as representative of anything Western is in no doubt cursor to the hatred of Igbos – agenda that is justified by religious bigotry. Unlike the West, where Islam is embraced by some members of the Yoruba tribe, the Igbos embraces with little or no conversion to Islam. Since the Igbos are culturally known for their migration pattern, they consequently adopt other cultures along their migration path. For the Igbos, their adoption and assimilation into the Hausa cultures and Muslim religion is very low. Igbos whole-hearted acceptance and affiliation with the Western missionaries continues bringing about disdain from some Muslims - extremists and now terrorist group, the Boko Haram.

These affiliations and developments fit the conspiracy that the Igbos are too embracing to Western cultures and religion and therefore a "sell-out" to the society especially their extreme-ideological religion with Sharia laws as its backbone. With a claim of affiliation to Israel, the Igbos are regarded as Zionists in character and form. These perceptions run deep across Muslims in Nigeria and around the world. Considering that the Igbos are Christians, and their affiliation with the West dates back to early missionaries in Nigeria, the Igbos represents anything and everything Western. Unlike the Yorubas that have Western education too, but show and manifest their own tradition and culture, the targeting of Yorubas have been minimum thus suggesting that the targeting of Igbos has a lot to do more with hate in the name of tribalism, the prejudice is against Igbos' entrepreneurship, and the association of Igbos to Judaism - Jewish religion and cultures; Christianity, which is "Western" to the average Muslim, and coupled with Igbos as being influenced by Western values, establishes some evidence why Igbos are targets of fundamentalists, and now Boko Haram. These reasons are as a result of a combination of myths and some established facts that some scholars have explored in their works.

While myths and conspiracy theories dominate debate on issues of importance that have socio-political implications for Nigeria, what the average Nigerians say on the streets about issues such as Boko Haram are essential to understanding why some pundits claim that the rhetoric of politicians and clerics – the leading voices in the propaganda against the West may be gaining ground, the fact that there is no plans or programs to counter the impact of these "brain-washing" messages are shocking to these observers and to a cross section of Nigerians. Opinion polls to measure the feelings of Nigerians about Boko Haram say a lot. The polls revealed these messages do affect the "conspiracy theorists" and their messages to win mind of not just Muslims, but Christians, as well. These views are revealing.

On the streets of Abuja, "Boko Haram is allegedly just a name given to the creation of few Northern politicians and elders to fight President Jonathan, whom they see as a Christian from the south that should not rule Nigeria," claims Jide Lawal. "I think that there's more to this Boko Haram nuisance than meets the eye," said Bello, a resident of Abuja.

While the Northern elders are blamed for the founding and sustenance of Boko Haram, some interviewees blame the West for Boko Haram. Some believe that the West even formulated the name. According to Zakari, a commuter in the city of Kano, one of the hubs of Islamic centers in Nigeria. "When it comes to the West, do not believe anything. I am suspecting that there are Western hands in the group." He backs up his argument with the conspiracy theorists that believe that while African leaders go to the West, sit and dine with Westerners, these people (West) sit down and plan years ahead of what they want to do or see happen not just in Africa but around the world."

He continued, I see the Western hand in Boko Haram since they have predicted that Nigeria will be a failed state by 2015." Like Jide, Zakari explains that the problem with the West is that they could never be trusted. Yes, the American People, the Europeans…on a person to person level, they are good people…..but when it come to their countries or their national interest, it is like the more they look into your eyes, the more lies you hear. They are very smart and have projections of what they want happen in 20 years not just in their countries but in Africa." He concludes that what happens in Africa and also in Nigeria regarding Western support for Boko Haram and their denial that they are helping Nigeria fight the insurgents is like the hand of Esau but the voice of Jacob in the Bible" exclaimed Bosco Oshodi. "Exactly! Unfortunately, we have very willing tools in the North due to poverty and illiteracy."

"The Oyibos (meaning the West in native dialect) have never meant well for the Black man. They feel they are superior to us in every way so when they see us rising, they do everything to suppress us," said Ibrahim. On the claim of Western influence and domination – all geared to subdue Africans, some of the interviewees dismissed the claim. One respondent said. "No, I don't agree with "the assertion that the West is out there to destroy the black man." He continued, "Do some soul –searching and just take a look to the leadership or the governance in Nigeria. Take for example since independence….. What have we achieved? We are busy maiming and killing ourselves; some politicians are robbing the country and yet we are comfortably playing the blame game. I do not care what anybody says, but let the truth be told, the buck stops here." He concludes, why are we complaining, after all, we were made by the same creator of other races. God …he gave us the same brain and same 24 hours in a day, so what are we talking about?"

In dismissing that the West is against the Black man, another interviewee said "Why are we complaining? How come China has become great even when the West never liked China and their people to grow at anything including competition?" The West never liked them too. What about Japan and South Korea? Japan cannot halt their production of Toyota to allow Kia to penetrate the market. China is already a great economic power because they looked inwards. So what stops Nigeria from using her abundant resources to become great?" asked Joshua. "It's like God's apprentices made us," replied Biola. This elicited laughter. Said Ibrahim: "Ajaokuta Steel Company is an example. It was meant to be the largest in Africa. ""Then corruption happened!" interjected Joshua. "Well, it was a conspiracy by the West. Ajaokuta Steel Limited was to enable us to become makers and exporters of steel.[13] The Russians were awarded the contract because the West did not like the idea, they started the project, suddenly the West became interested and was awarded the civil engineering work, and then the cold war started. The West used their civil engineering companies to frustrate the project. Africa is the largest market for Western automobiles, so if Nigeria begins to produce steel, they will lose the market and that was why they conspired to retard the growth of the project," said Ibrahim. "Ah, your school fees were not in vain. You're making sense," joked Biola.

"So you now see why the Boko Haram thing can as well be a conspiracy? Nigeria is blessed in every sense of the word, and if it is allowed to develop will become a big threat to the West and so the best thing is to destabilize her, not from outside but from within; set them up against themselves and fragment the country, Joshua remarked.[14]

Joshua explained that it is not just the West, Arabs and Nigerians are aiding in the destruction of the country that took life and death for Nigeria's fathers of Independence to build. He remarked, "Kano, Jos and Kaduna would have been a strong business corridor but look at what has happened! According to him an average Nigerian will prefer to get N1million as his own share even if the country will lose N10 million in the process. "It is that bad. I know of a Lebanese businessman owing PHCN N50, 000 but was willing to bribe them with N40, 000 instead of paying the N50, 000 and getting a receipt." He expressed disappointment with the system with laws that are not followed or enforced. " This is aiding a foreigner to defraud us. Will a White guy allow a Black man to defraud his government?" asked Sani. "Impossible,"[15] he replied

These conversations tell one thing that even though the majority of Nigerians, mainly Southern youth would like to migrate to the United States as Pew Survey revealed, the sentiments that often are created against the West runs deep among Southerners. These conspiracy theories as alleged are often given attention and propagated by both Muslim and Christian elites mainly politicians and some religious clerics in the North.

A source told the author how as a teenager and a first year college student in the 90s, he was given a free video depicting the West as unreliable and untruthful. The documentary video titled "Double-Speak" according to the student has been duplicated as many times as possible and distributed to both Muslim and Christian youths. The lessons in the video according to the source is about conspiracy theories and events in the United States that depict the United States as fabricating events to empower and also "rule the world." While these conspiracy theories exist without any counter information by the State Department at the time, things have since changed in the Arab world with anti-United States counter propaganda machinery, but not that I am aware in Africa. Sources disclosed that programs are on the way to use the media and other communication tools to dissuade youths in Northern Nigeria from their view of the West as "evil" that has been rife in the North until Boko Haram assumed that name and started their campaign to live up to what they have preached and taught in their Mosque to hate the West.

Chapter 4

Boko Haram – Why Igbos (Southeastern Christians) are the Easy Targets of Fundamentalist Groups in Nigeria?

Living among Muslims indicates that the extremist exploiting religion purposely for their selfish ends; what they say or do does not represent the religion's tenets. In Ghana and Togo history indicates Christians and Muslims rarely clash. Why Igbo Christians are always targeted by religious violence in the North remains puzzling. "Why is it that whenever there is rioting in the Middle East, Palestine or in the streets of Paris over one controversial Islamic issue with the West or the Israelis, Igbos in the North are always the target? – An unanimous source asked.[1] A good example was the political unrest that rocked Egypt after Morsi's ouster in July 3, 2013 by "military coup" - following massive public protests. When he was removed from office, the Muslim Brotherhood demonstrated wanting the military to restore Morsi to power.

As with other political and religious events in the Muslim world that have their ripple effects in Nigeria, more than 4000 Muslims youth rallied in northern Nigeria in solidarity with Muslim Brotherhood demanding the return of Egypt's Islamist former president Mohamed Morsi, ousted by the military.[2]

These events are not far to explain the role religion plays in politics. Religion may explain some of the reasons why in a secular state such as Nigeria; when issues that are purely political that has nothing to do with religious, when questioned by either Christians or Muslims, for example, is perceived often as a confrontation to Christianity or Islam, and in most times triggers anger and animosity some of them spilling over to violence and bloodbath on the streets. However, considering that Nigeria in the North has countries that are Muslim nations and with Nigeria's open boundaries, extremists from neighboring countries have easily infiltrated into Nigeria through her unprotected borders. Nigeria easily attracts extremists from neighboring countries that freely migrate to boost jihadist movement and "fight the holy war."[3]

Nigeria is the most populated country in Africa. It is also an economic powerhouse of the region, and Africa's third largest economy. These are both Nigeria's strengths and weaknesses. With internal security threats by those exploiting her diversity to cause trouble instead of concentrating on beneficial policies, Nigeria's attention is diverted to defending itself from internal conflicts when the concentration of efforts should be how to defend itself from external enemies while strategizing to gain investors to develop the economy. These threats from within and external come in the form of tribal and religious clashes. Executors, who come in different styles and forms as non-Nigerians can migrate to the country without identification, they wear robes of brotherhood, easily absorbed into the system, using religion as a disguise to destabilize Nigeria.

The Igbos, often victims of attacks are stereotyped as "the Jews of Africa." No studies show whether those affiliations have any roles in the ethnic targeting of Igbos in the name of religious riots that sometimes Western policy on Middle East or perceived as anti-Islamic by fundamentalists often trigger the massacre of the Igbos. Speaking before the British Parliament in April 2013, former governor of Abia State, Chief Orji Kalu disclosed that Igbo have suffered in Nigeria, Kalu recalled the Igbo massacres in Kano, in 1980; Maiduguri, in 1982; Yola, in 1984; Gombe, in 1985; Kaduna, in 1986; Bauchi, in 1991; Funtua, in 1993; Kano, in 1994; Damboa, in 2000 and the Apo 6 massacre, in 2005. He said that although the slaughter of people by Boko Haram is yet to be documented, there could be no question that a disproportionate percentage of the thousands of victims, dead or maimed or permanently impoverished, comprised of Igbos.

According to him, "Nigerian Muslims who had been provoked not by any direct misconduct by the Igbo, but perhaps because the Prophet Mohammed was insulted in Denmark by some European artist or because Allah's name had been taken in vain in Los Angeles by an American satirist" have killed Igbo. He said that it was in order to address these issues that *Njiko Igbo*, a pan-Igbo group was formed. [4]

This notion of connecting Igbos to the Jewish people of Israel could be traced to the tenets of the Hamitic hypothesis which posited that certain superior groups and tribes came from northeast Africa or beyond including Israel and survived in sub-Saharan Africa in a degenerate form.[5] Horton, was absorbed to the idea that "The Igbo could trace their origins back to the Lost Tribes of Israel, and that the Igbo language was heavily influenced by Hebrew."[6]   The claim to Jewish heritage is also founded by George T. Basden, who first arrived in

Igbo territory in 1900. Baden, a scholar and an ethnographer is recognized as a leading expert on the subject of Igbos and their Jewish origin[7]. Elizabeth Isichei also offered insights into the origin and history of Igbo people. [8]

Olaudah Equiano's biography described the analogies between Jewish customs, law, belief and those of Igbos.[9] John Ogilby account revealed there were indeed Jews and Jewish or Israeli customs in West Africa; which Tudor Parfitt, affirmed that Jewish customs were to be found in the Igbo areas of West Africa. "To this day, for some Igbos, the idea that "Igbo" and "Hebrew" (or ivri) are one and the same word and that the two languages are closely related is quite widespread."[10] Former the Premier of Eastern Nigeria, Dr. Michael Okpara, a renowned Igbo leader, he was accused of declaring himself "an Israeli" during the Biafra war that coincided with the six-day Arab-Israeli conflict of June 1967. The Biafran war was read as Northern-Southern confrontation, same as the Arab-Israeli war. Whether it served right was yet to be established by history; it is not proven whether Jews actually helped Igbos in war.

In the 21st century, Igbos are being perceived as the "Jews of Africa." It could also be due their successes in business and politics which often compared to Jews have similar qualities to assimilate easily wherever they find themselves and do well. With a small homeland with economic gains through ingenious efforts, people in spaces where Igbos migrate are often very uncomfortable with "these immigrants" and their success stories. For the evidence that Igbos migrates to their "lands" and quickly gain economic control does not reduce prejudice. Igbos' boasted dynamism in adapting to their new environment and sometimes-taking charge of businesses in their new homeland makes the Igbos suspects, thus leading to tensions. An example of Igbos' ingenious survival instinct was at the end of Nigeria civil war (July 6, 1967 – January 15, 1970). The Nigeria Civil War, also known as the Nigeria-Biafra War, was as a result of attempted secession of the southeastern provinces of Nigeria as the self-proclaimed Republic of Biafra.

At the end of the civil war, every Igbo man was allowed to withdraw only $25 pounds (even with $1 million pounds in the account) as part of the "reconciliation" program. The Igbos in spite of setback has since rebounded economically through their individual and group's self-determination. The strength of the Igbos does not go well with the other tribes especially in the Muslim North where rural nomadic lifestyle and agriculture are ways of life. The courage of the Igbos and their entrepreneurship exacerbate the discrimination.

For some states in the South that have established networks and collaborations with the Jewish state, including organized pilgrimages, business trips, agricultural and educational exchange programs to Israel do not improve Igbos relationship with Muslim fundamentalists. "Many observers believe that the Ibos' high level of education, coupled with the extremely high number of managerial and professional posts they occupied, generated intense envy among the Nigerians." Jeffrey D. Blum was reporting on the visit US State Department six-man fact-finding mission in 1969 to examine the needs of both Nigeria and Biafra and to make recommendations to the U.S. government about the necessary forms and amount of possible aid. Senator Charles E. Goodell (R.-N.Y.), was the head of the delegation while his administrative assistant--Charles W. Dunn--was in charge of the mission's diplomatic aspects.[11]

The present situation at the Gaza Strip with killings of young Palestinians, the expanding Israeli occupation of Palestinian land and the threat of war with Iran, the movie trailer or cartoon of Islamic leader in faraway countries of Middle East, United States and Europe do cause reactions in Nigeria from Muslim groups that target Igbos whenever rioting breaks out in Europe and the Middle East.

The growing population of Igbo Jews of Nigeria - known as the "Benei-Yisrael," who claimed that they traced their origin from the biblical tribes of Gad, Asher, Dan, and Naphtali does not build friendship with jihadists. These Igbos traced their migration through Syria, Portugal and Libya into West Africa around 740 C.E to Nigeria. They claimed that they were joined by more Jewish immigrants from Portugal and Libya in 1484 and 1667 respectively.[12]

These claims and the counterarguments notwithstanding, in spite of the British colonial powers preference to hand over the premiership of Nigeria to the North after Nigeria's independence in 1960, Christianity remains a bond between the West and Southerners in Nigeria. The travels and evangelization trips by missionaries dating back to more than two centuries bring uncertainties and mistrust between Muslims and Christians. For the extremists (fundamentalists) in the North who are never short of expressing their goals and unapologetic for "holy war" to spread their ideologies beyond their Northern borders, see Igbos as easy target for this their disdain of the Western culture and values.

When these fundamentalists perceived that their religion is under attack by the West through policies or through media framing, they often find easy target to avenge those angers, and Igbos mainly living in their abode (since Igbos as the Jews are migrants and the Igbos perceived association with the Jews) often project the Igbos as their easy targets. Fundamentalists' agenda are always manifested on T.V, rallies, and even "religious events" where they reveal their disenchantment with the West. They also condemn the secularity of Nigeria states. Their unrelenting goal is to resist any values that corruption their culture as they find convenient using Sharia to back up their arguments.

Nigeria's fundamentalists no doubt share the same ideologies with their peers around the world, in particular countries in the Middle East where extreme religious beliefs have torn countries apart. In Nigeria's situation such attempts have persisted, however, authorities and the people have resisted the fundamentalists from using religion to achieve their other objectives of destroyed the country by introducing extreme theocracy.

Boko Haram (Western education is sin) currently operating in the country is a mutation of fundamentalist groups from the past trying to achieve their goals with new name, new technology and global collaboration from Al-Qaida network around the Mediterranean and Middle East. They walk from the sidelines onto center stage, using religion as a frame of reference even as they take anti-religion and anti-Christian actions. One thing that fundamentalists want to do is play big roles to push their agenda through at costs that may hurt and haunt others in the long run. Another feature fundamentalists share is fear of any kind of change, especially in modern secular culture that is Nigeria.

Chapter 5

Boko Haram – Timeline of Terror Attacks in Nigeria

It was August 26, 2011; timeline 11.00 a.m. when a suicide bomber drove a vehicle-borne improvised explosive device (VBIED) into the U.N. headquarters in Abuja, Nigeria. As he did the long driveway to his target, the vehicle loaded with a 100-pound bomb raised no suspicion to passers-bye and security agents patrolling the space until the car crashed into security barriers very close to the UN building's reception area. The vehicle loaded with the bomb exploded and tore apart the structure, which housed about 26 different U.N. agencies. On a count, 23 were dead, and 80 others injured. Boko Haram, an Islamist group, claimed responsibility.

Boko Haram had until this incident targeted institutions perceived by the group as symbols of "Western education and knowledge"; places of Christian worships, government officials and security forces, but the attack by the insurgents of the UN building marked the first time in Nigeria that Boko Haram targeted an international organization. However, the attack was not surprising to national and international intelligence agency who long believed that Boko Haram, which draws inspiration from Afghanistan,'s Taliban, has links with Al-Qaeda in the Middle East, and AL- Qaeda in the Islamic Maghreb (AQIM). Boko Haram that draws inspiration from these terror groups has shown that it is capable of executing attacks beyond its domestic operation in Nigeria.

While Boko Haram had targeted its suicide bombing to churches, public gathering places such as market place, motor packs and beer parlors; it has also attacked clerics who opposed its espoused extreme Islamic ideologies. In fact, while the introduction of an extreme form of Sharia laws and Islamization of Nigeria are the group's goal, its other targets included attacks on government officials and security forces. Even with these random bombings of targets, the attack on the United Nation's building marked the first time the terrorist group targeted an international organization in Nigeria. Another terror attack on the soil of Africa was the Al-Qaeda bombings on the U.S. Embassies in Dar es Salem, Tanzania and Nairobi, Kenya in 1998. Those terror attacks killed 224, including 212 Africans, and 12 Americans; more than 5,000 were injured[1]

Therefore, the attack on the UN headquarters at Abuja Nigeria reawakened the experience of the bloody attacks - the US embassy bombings in Tanzania and Kenya, reminding the world that terrorism is alive. The investigation into the attacks on the US Embassies traced the violence to Al-Qaeda. Similarly, the result of the investigation led to the declaration of Osama Bin Laden as the Most Wanted Person on the FBI list. In the same way AQIM-linked terrorists were believed to have played a key role in the attack in September 2012 on the U.S. diplomatic mission in Benghazi, Libya, that killed four Americans, including U.S. Ambassador Chris Stevens."[2] Therefore, the attack of the UN headquarters in Abuja, Nigeria confirmed the links between Nigeria's Boko Haram and Al-Qaeda in Middle East and AL- Qaeda in the IslamicMaghreb(AQIM)

Boko Haram, has attacked Christian churches as well as institutions that represented Western values as they claimed from their name, Boko Haram meaning in Hausa language "Western education is sacrilegious." Like the Al-Qaeda terror group, Boko Haram has masterminded and executed highly planned military-style bombings. Its combats with Nigeria's security forces revealed the extent of their military training and their sophistication of weaponry. Like the Al-Qaeda in the Middle East and Al- Qaeda in the Islamic Maghreb (AQIM), Boko Haram has successfully executed simultaneous attacks on its intended targets leaving casualties estimated at 3,600.[3] With Boko Haram's claims to these attacks and their pronouncement of an unending battle till its objectives are accomplished, there seems to be no end to the terror that the group is ready to unleash on Nigeria state and people. .

President Goodluck Jonathan, during an interview with CNN while on China visit in July 2013, assured Nigerians and the global community that Boko Haram would be history in three months, but the repeat attacks on their targets – churches, public spaces where non-Muslims assemble, government officials and security forces have not stopped. While it seems the group's virtuosity has been reduced, there are still strong feelings among non-Muslims in Nigeria that Boko Haram apart from wanting Islamic laws in place across Nigeria, it is also trying to trigger clashes between Christians and Muslims. As pundits predicted, Book Haram's objective is a failed Nigeria state.

In retrospect, Boko Haram was founded in 2002 by Mohammed Yusuf. He was killed by government forces in 2009. However, before then – precisely between 2002 and 2009, there were hardly any open confrontations or acts of terrorism associated with the group. However, intelligence reports indicated that the group was acquiring arms and at the same time having contacts with international terror groups, the Al-Qaeda in the Middle East and the Somalia–based Al-Qaeda in the Islamic Maghreb. When the State Security Services stepped in to investigate the suspicious activities of the group, clashes ensued between the Federal agents and the jihadists. Boko Haram members used ammunitions as well as poison-spiced bows and arrows to attack Federal agents. The aftermath of the confrontation by Boko Haram with the Federal Joint Military Forces left more than 700 people dead.

Boko Haram's leader Mohammed Yusuf was finally captured during the raid. He later died while under the custody of the Nigeria security force, marking the escalation of attacks by the terror group that is in line with its extremist ideology, extolling a version of Islam where any interaction with Western society is considered a sin.[4] It also marked the full execution of its fundamentalist ideologies which include the Islamization of Nigeria as well as targeting individuals, religious and tribal groups that the group perceives as a threat to its core Islamic form of sharia.

As evidence from the glossaries of Boko Haram attacks and bloodbath in Nigeria from 2009 to the present revealed, the group that draws its inspiration from the Afghanistan Taliban has been relentless in its attacks on its targets. Innocent Nigerians, mainly Christians of Igbo extract, have been the target of the group while the government officials and security forces mobilized to dislodge the terror group were also targeted. With another splinter group, *Ansaru*, Boko Haram continues to target state and religious institutions, kidnap, and kill foreigners in Nigeria.

In March 2013, another of Boko Haram's splinter group *Jama a'tu Ansaru Muslimina Fi Baladis Sudan*, translated as "Vanguards for the protection of Muslims in Black Africa" claimed it killed 7 foreigners, the hostages they seized on February 7, 2013 from a construction company. The dead were a Briton, an Italian, a Greek and 4 Lebanese workers. The terror group showed screen shots of dead hostages which it claimed were all Christians.[5]

While the Federal Government was under pressure to inaugurate a presidential committee to examine the circumstances of Boko Haram's insurgents and consider the possibility of granting amnesty to its members, one of the conditions was that it lay down arms and come to the negotiating table. The group has since dismissed the idea of meeting with the presidential committee even as the plea for amnesty by political leaders, traditional rulers and clerics from the North divided the country. The majority of the population believed that Boko Haram members should be punished to the last letters of the law (instead of negotiation) to avoid setting a bad precedent that might motivate wannabe terrorists.

Meanwhile, Boko Haram through its leader has indicated that the Federal government should apologize to the group and ask for forgiveness for arresting, attacking, and killing Boko Haram members. The group continues to attack even at the time this book was going to press. Despite the huge offensive by the Joint Military Task Force, with 2000 men and women of the armed forces on Boko Haram's trail, the group continues to engage in sporadic attacks and leaves casualties in its tracks. Boko Haram rebuffed the idea of amnesty claiming that it is the federal government that should apologize to the group for killing its members, arresting and detaining others including members of their families. In essence, the group has rebuffed truce, while it continued to attack innocent citizens, foreign workers, and institutions of the state and the federal governments. With more than 2000 Joint Military Task Forces on the ground following the order issued by the president to dislodge the terror group, reports in the media suggested that Boko Haram has accepted to lay down arms.

When on July 12, 2013 Boko Haram declared a cease –fire and sought a truce with the Federal Government, it was not clear whether the terror group was playing to the gallery or being sincere in its decision to stop its bloodbath. The terror group has made such moves unofficially previously, only to return and intensify its attacks. Since, it was not clear whether the group was overwhelmed by the offensive of the Joint Military Force that was set up by the President to flush out the members of the group, the Director of Defense Information, Brigadier-General Chris Olukolade said at a press conference that the military operation to dislodge Boko Haram and rid the North-East part of the country of terrorists was on track and would continue in spite of the truce requested by the terror group. Brigadier –General Olukode said, "As for the operational aspect, it will be maintained. So far, there has been no directive to stop the operation. We will not succumb to any deception whether ceasefire or not until otherwise directed by government." [6]

General Chris Olukolade denied receiving information either from his top commander or from Boko Haram leaders, who are still hiding from bullets and shelling unleashed by the Joint Military Task Force. With air and ground assaults, Boko Haram was reported to have fled to Border Mountains in neighboring Niger and Mali. Some members, it was learned, melted into the civilian population while the majority escaped into the mountainous regions of neighboring countries of Niger and Chad. However, pundits have indicated that this pattern the group has used previously only to return and unleash more damages and bloodbath.

As evidence show s, more than 12, 000 have been killed by Boko Haram jihadists is an underestimation, since some deaths were not accounted for and given the media coverage or reported eye witness accounts from which these figures were generated. With continuous attacks in the month of July 2013 when this book was about to go to press, it is evident that Nigeria has witnessed more casualties from terror than was witnessed in 9/11 when terrorists rammed hijacked planes into the World Trade Center leading to the Coalition Forces' invasion of Iraq and later Afghanistan.

BOKO HARAM & VIOLENCE – TIMELINE OF TERROR INCIDENTS

September 23, 2003 – Clashes between security forces and Islamic militants left 29 dead.[7]

February 20, 2004 – Nigeria arrests official of a British-based Muslim charity in connection with Islamic uprising in Nigeria.[8]

October 8, 2004 – Three police officers killed, 12 abducted by Boko Haram in Northeastern Nigeria.[9]

July 26, 2006 – Bomb explodes in Maiduguri – Islamic sect member killed.[10]

July 25 – 29, 2009 – Five-day clashes between security forces and Boko Haram members led to loss of more than 800 lives in Maiduguri, Bauchi, Nubi and Kaduna. Security operatives had gone to Boko Haram following investigation that revealed that the jihadist group was acquiring arms and has links to Al-Qaeda in Maghreb (AQIM). [11]

July 25, 2009 – 39 people killed in Nigeria clashes between Boko Haram and Federal Agents in Bauchi, Northeastern Nigeria. Clashes reportedly began after dozens of men armed with guns and explosives attacked a police station.[12]

July 26, 2009 – 42 dead as Taliban-sect and police clash in Bauchi.[13]

July 26, 2009 – Bauchi relaxes curfew, 52 confirmed dead.[14]

July 27, 2009 – Deadly clashes spread and continued. Many dead in Nigeria market blast. Boko Haram killed 55 people bringing to 150 the number of deaths in the two-day wave of violence.[15]

July 27, 2009 – 52 Boko Haram members killed. Two police officers and a soldier killed in Boko Haram's violence in Bauchi. [16]

July 27, 2009 - Scores of people were killed in Northern Nigeria after three attacks by Islamist militants, taking the total killed in two days of violence to 150. Armed clashes continued. Armed with cutlasses and guns – Boko Haram slashed the neck of police officer near the Emir's palace in Maiduguri.[17]

July 28, 2009 – Army shelled Yusuf's compound in Maiduguri, and flushed out two of his followers. Killed were dozens of people. Yusuf was arrested as he hid in his father-in-law's goat pen and taken into police custody.[18]

July 29, 2009 – Mohammed Yusuf dead while in police custody, Abubakar Shakur takes over Boko Haram's leadership after Yusuf's death.[19]

July 29, 2009 - Nigerian police freed about 100 women and children held by Boko Haram in a building in Maiduguri. Official documents and personal items found on the location showed Boko Haram members migrated from neighboring countries of Chad and Niger. [20]

July 30, 2009 – Security officials in Maiduguri claimed to have killed Yusuf's deputy Abubakar Shakur, but later police identified wrong person and found out that Shakur is alive.[21]

August 2, 2009 – 780 bodies were collected in Maiduguri, Borno State and buried in three mass graves.[22]

August 3, 2009 – Police confirmed 55 killed in Bauchi, 45 in and around Potiskun, Yobe State and 4 in Wudil, Kano State. [23]

September 7, 2010 – Boko Haram attacked Bauchi prison and freed prisoners. 712 out of the 759 inmates at the Bauchi Prisons escaped.[24]

September 22, 2010 – Boko Haram claimed killings in Borno.[25]

December 25, 2010 – Christmas Eve attack on Churches in Jos and Maiduguri. Boko Haram claimed responsibility for the attacks as "revenge to atrocities committed against Muslims in Kaduna and Plateau States.[26]

December 31, 2010 – Abuja attack: Four people were killed, including a pregnant woman, and 26 were injured.[27]

January 19, 2011 - Boko Haram attacked Dala Alemderi ward in Maiduguri metropolis, Bornu State. Four people were killed.[28]

March 8, 2011 - Briton and two Italians died in a failed rescue attempt by security forces as they attempted to rescue the hostages held in Sokoto. Seven people died in the operation.[29]

March 29, 2011 - Police thwarted a plot to bomb an [ANPP] election rally" in Maiduguri, Bornu State. The threat was blamed on Boko Haram.[30]

April 1, 2011 - Boko Haram bombings in the northeastern state of Bornu continued. It targeted areas that had supported President Goodluck Jonathan in his winning the presidential election. Police station in Bauchi State was also attacked.[30]

April 9, 2011 - A polling center at Unguwar Doki of Maiduguri metropolis was bombed. Over ten people were injured.[31]

April 15, 2011 – The office of the Independent National Electoral Commission in Maiduguri was bombed, and several people were shot in a separate incident on the same day. Authorities suspected Boko Haram.[32]

April 15, 2011 - Two people, among them a soldier, were killed; seven others were injured when unknown gunmen opened fire on residents in the city's Gwange distract.[33]

April 20, 2011 - Boko Haram killed a Muslim cleric and ambushed many police officers in Maiduguri.[34]

April 22, 2011 – Boko Haram breaks into prison in Yola, Adamawa, and frees 14 Prisoners.[35]

May 28, 2011 - 15 people killed by bombing by Boko Haram, a day before President Goodluck Jonathan was inaugurated on May 29, 2011.[36]

May 29, 2011 - An explosion at a market in Bauchi, east of Zaria, killed 13 people and wounded 20.[38]

May 29, 2011 - In Zuba, outside the capital Abuja, a blast at a beer parlor killed two and wounded 11. May 30, 2011 – Two more bombs went off in Maiduguri and Zaria. These terror attacks were following the explosions that killed 15 people on May 28, 2011, a day before President Goodluck Jonathan was inaugurated.[39]

June 1, 2011 - A German Engineer, Edgar Fritz Raupach, held hostage by gunmen since January 26, 2011, was killed by his captors as the Nigerian security forces stormed their hideout located at Danbare suburb, along Gwarzo highway, in Kano. Six people died during the encounter including the five sect members and a woman, while three soldiers sustained injuries from a blast during the operations.[40]

June 7, 2011 - A gunman believed to be from the Boko Haram Muslim sect has shot dead a prominent cleric from a rival sect in northern Nigeria. Ibrahim Birkuti criticized Boko Haram for killing dozens of security agents and near the city of Maiduguri.[41]

June 16, 2011 – Boko Haram's Abuja police headquarters bombing. Two people were confirmed killed in the blast: the driver of the vehicle, which exploded, and a police officer who got into the car at a security checkpoint. Later taken away from the scene were five body bags.[42]

June 26, 2011 – Bombing of a beer garden in Maiduguri. 25 people killed and 12 wounded in the terror attack.[43]

June 26, 2011 - University of Maiduguri shut down as Boko Haram's linked-killings increased in the University City.[44]

July 10, 2011 – All Christian Fellowship Church in Suleija, Niger State was bombed, and three people at the location were killed. Boko Haram also used Improvised Explosive Devices at political rally and the offices of the Independent Electoral Commission in Suleija and Dakwa village, Bwari. The explosives killed unaccounted number of people. About 200 explosives were retrieved at the time of arrest of four suspects in the attack, later charged to court.[45]

August 25, 2011 – Boko Haram suicide bombers attacked United Nations' Nigeria headquarters at Abuja left 23 dead and scores of people injured.[46]

November 4, 2011 – Damaturu bombing. 63 killed in a terror attack claimed by Boko Haram, Nine churches were also attacked and burnt down. The attacks followed a triple suicide bomb attacks on a military headquarters in Maiduguri in Bornu state.[47]

December 25, 2011 - Suicide bombers left 26 worshippers dead in a church blast. A series of bomb attacks, including two on Christmas Day church services left 40 people dead and many injured. Boko Haram claimed the attacks including attack on St Theresa's Church in Madalla, near the capital Abuja that killed 35. A second explosion shortly after hit a church in the central city of Jos. A police officer died during gunfire. Three attacks in northern Yobe State left four people dead. Two hit the town of Damaturu, and a third struck Gadaka. Yobe state known as the epicenter of violence between security forces and Boko Haram militants. [48]

December 25, 2011 - Abul Qaqa, Boko Haram spokesman claimed responsibility for the attacks in Maiduguri, Damaturu and Potiskum. We carried out the attacks to avenge the killings of our brothers by the security forces in 2009. We will continue to wage war against the Nigerian state until we abolish the secular system and establish an Islamic state.[49]

December 26, 2011 – Two suspects in the Christmas Church suicide bombing that killed 26 arrested.[50]

December 30, 2011 – President Goodluck Jonathan in a meeting with the National Security Adviser (NSA), General Andrew Azazi (rtd.); the Inspector General of Police (IGP), Hafiz Ringim and other security chiefs at the Presidential Villa, Abuja. President Jonathan ordered top security chiefs to track down the sponsors of Boko Haram. As a follow up to ensuring that lives and property were secured, on December 31, 2011 - President Goodluck Jonathan declared a state of emergency in the northeast and two other regions in Nigeria on Dec. 31, in a bid to contain a growing insurgency by Boko Haram.[51]

January 3, 2012 – A Nigerian newspaper published a warning from Boko Haram after series of Church bombings giving Christians ultimatum (three days) to leave northern Nigeria.[52]

January 5, 2012 - As people gathered to mourn the death of people earlier killed by gunmen identified as the same attackers at Mubi- they opened fire and killed 18 at the funeral.[53]

January 5, 2012 - A Christian couple was shot dead in the night in Maiduguri.[54]

Boko Haram's spokesman, Abu Qaqa confirmed by telephone interview that the terror group was responsible for many attacks including Church shooting in Gombe on January 5, 2012 which killed 6 people "The Gombe attack on Deeper Life Church, the attack on the Igbos in Mubi and Yola - mainly the targets of Boko Haram in these attacks were carried out by us."[55]

January 7, 2012 – Thousands of Christians, mainly Igbos begin to flee northern Nigeria after dozens were killed in a series of attacks by Islamist militants who issued an ultimatum to Christians to leave the predominantly Muslim-populated states or be killed. Christians flee as they were afraid for their lives, and security was not guaranteed.[56]

January 7, 2012 - After the ultimatum expired, Boko Haram attacked in towns in four states in northeastern Nigeria leaving 37 people dead.[57]

January 9, 2012 - President Goodluck Jonathan revealed a gloomy picture of the membership and activities of the deadly Islamic sect, Boko Haram. Speaking at an inter-denominational church service to mark the 2012 Armed Forces Remembrance Day celebration at the National Christian Centre, President Jonathan disclosed that Boko Haram has successfully infiltrated the three arms of government at the national level.[58]

January 11, 2012 - Boko Haram members opened fire on a commuter van full of Igbo passengers leaving the north, killing four of the passengers, at a filling station in Potiskum, Yobe State.[59]

Jan. 20, 2012 – 185 killed including residents, journalists, 29 police officers in a series of blasts, including a suicide bombing and shootings in Kano. Affected were three city police stations, a police barrack and home of Assistant Inspector General of Police in charge of the region, local offices if the State Security Services and Immigration Department. Boko Haram claimed responsibility for the attacks. [60]

January 23, 2012 – Indian and Nepalese killed in Kano blasts.[61]

January 28, 2012 - "Eleven Boko Haram (BH) members were killed by Joint Military Taskforce (JTF) in Maiduguri after a shootout with the sect members at a checkpoint during stop and search operation.[62]

March 30, 2012 – 4 dead. Boko Haram claims responsibility.[63]

July 2011 – The Mayor of Makary, Cameroon's Far North Region, Mr. Abba Djidda Alahdji was killed by Boko Haram because of his suspected ties with a Nigerian police commissioner, raising fears about how far the sect members could stretch their wrath. [64]

January 12, 2012 - More than 100 people killed as security agents confronts Boko Haram in the Nigeria northern city of Kano in what was described as the deadliest confrontation by Nigeria security forces with members of the sect.[65]

February 8, 2012 - Suicide Bombing at the Army Headquarters in Kaduna. A man wearing a military uniform blew himself up outside the barracks. Boko Haram claims responsibility.[66]

February 16, 201 - 119 prisoners were released, one warden killed in North Central Nigeria after break in to the prison masterminded by Boko Haram terrorists.[67]

February 19, 2012 – Bomb explodes near church in the town of Suleija on the edge of the Nigerian capital Abuja. Five people were wounded as a result of the attack. [68]

February 26, 2012 – A suicide bomber drives a car packed with explosives into a church in Jos, killing six Christians and wounding 38. Boko Haram claimed the attack. Christian youths beat two Muslims to death in revenge.[69]

March 8, 2012 - Italian Engineer Franco Lamolinara and Briton Christopher McManus, abducted in 2011 by a splinter group were killed during a rescue mission led by the British to free the hostages. Boko Haram denied role in the kidnapping.[70]

March 11, 2012 - A Boko Haram suicide bomber killed three civilians in a bombing outside a church in Jos. Reprisal attacks against Muslims by Christian youths kill at least 10 people.[71]

April 8, 2012 - A car bomb explodes on Easter Sunday near a church in the northern town of Kaduna, killing at least 36 people and badly wounding 13.[72]

April 26, 2012 - The editor of This Day confirmed that a suicide bomber drove a jeep into the newspaper's office in Abuja, killing two people. [73]

April 29, 2012 – Gunmen open fire and throw homemade bombs at a lecture theatre in the University of Kano used for Christian fellowship. Church of Christ in Maiduguri is also attacked in northeast Maiduguri. 19 people were killed in the attacks, blamed by police on Boko Haram.
[74]

April 30, 2012 - 16 people were killed and six others in serious condition as Boko Haram attacked Christian worship holding a service at the Lecture Theatre used as a place of worship by Christians at Bayero University, Kano.[75]

April 30, 2012 - A Boko Haram suicide bomber killed 11 people and wounded more than 20 in an attack on a police convoy in Jalingo, the capital of Taraba state.[76]

May 31, 2012 - During a Joint Task Force raid on a Boko Haram's den, it was reported that 6 gunmen and a German hostage were killed. Al-Qaeda in the Islamic Maghreb (AQIM) claims responsibility for the kidnapping.[77]

June 3, 2012 - A Boko Haram suicide bomber killed 15 people in an attack on a church in Yelwa, on the outskirts of the northern city of Bauchi. Boko Haram claimed responsibility through spokesperson Abu Qaqa.[78]

June 8, 2012 - A Boko Haram suicide bomber killed four people in an attack outside a police station in Maiduguri.[79]

June 10, 2012 – Three gunmen sprayed bullets at the congregation in a church in Biu Town, in northeastern Borno state. Also on the same date in June 10, 2012 - suicide bomber drives a car to the entrance of the Christ Chosen Church in Jos and blows it up. Three people killed in the attack outside the church. Youths attack bystanders in retaliation, killing two people.[80]

July 12, 2012 – Boko Haram Kills 130 innocent villagers. On the other side, Boko Haram accused the Joint Military Task Force for the high number of casualties following military attack to flush out members of the group in their camps. Eyewitnesses reported the insurgents resisted the task force, and in open air battle many civilians were killed.[81]

July 13, 2012 - A suicide bomber killed five people in an attack at a mosque in Maiduguri.[82]

June 16, 2012 – Boko Haram attacks police headquarters in Abuja.[83]

June 17, 2012 – Suicide bombers strike three churches in Kaduna. 50 people were killed. About 131 people were injured by the violence -

the third weekend in a row in which Boko Haram has carried out bombings on churches according to Red Cross. Two of the blasts happened in the Wusasa and Sabon-Gari districts of the town of Zaria, and a third hit the nearby city of Kaduna, the state capital. About 130 bodies found in Plateau State. They victims were presumed killed by Boko Haram members.[84]

June 23, 2012 – Boko Haram prison break – Frees 40 prison inmates.[85]

July 26, 2012 – Suspected members of Boko Haram killed two Indians.[86]

Aug. 3, 2012 - A Boko Haram suicide bomber wounded several people in a failed attack outside of a mosque in Potiskum. Emir's body gad and mosque aid hurt in the suicide attack [87]

August 5, 2012 - Boko Haram suicide bomber killed six military men and two civilians in Nigeria's northern city of Damaturu.[88]

August 8, 2012 - At least 19 worshippers at Deeper Life Church were killed when members of a radical Islamist sect Boko Haram opened indiscriminate fire at an evangelical church in Kogi Northern Nigeria during a service. Boko Haram after the attack on the church issued a statement that claimed responsibility for the Sunday August 5, 2012 attack in Damataru. [89]

Aug. 15, 2012 - A suicide bomber killed three civilians in a failed attempt to target a vehicle belonging to the Joint Task Force in Maiduguri. Also on August 15, 2012 - Four -3 injured in failed suicide attempt. [90]

September 19, 2012 – The spokesman for Islamist militant group Boko Haram, Abu Qaqa was killed. [91]

Sept. 23, 2012 - September 23, 2012 - A suicide car bomber blew self-up at St John's Catholic Church, Bauchi, in a remote part of northern Nigeria, killing a woman and child and wounding at least 22 other people. [92]

October 3, 2012 – 46 persons, mostly students from three tertiary institutions in Mubi town, Adamawa State, were killed by gunmen suspected to be members of Boko Haram. Students shot dead by Boko Haram members were from Federal Polytechnic, the School of Health Technology and the Adamawa State University, all in Mubi. [93]

October 28, 2012 - A Boko Haram suicide bomber drove an explosives-packed jeep into St. Rita Catholic Church in Ungwar Yero city of Kaduna metropolis killing at least eight people and wounding over 100. [94]

Nov. 25, 2012 - A Boko Haram suicide bomber rammed a bus packed with explosives into the church during services at the Jaji military barracks in Kaduna state. The blasts killed 11 people and wounded over 30. [95]

May 5, 2013 – Boko Haram kills four members of Ibadan Foodstuff Sellers Association.[96]

May 7, 2013 - At least 55 killed and 105 inmates freed in coordinated attacks on army barracks, prison, and police posts in Bama town.[97]

May 17, 2013 - Nigeria's military declared a 24-hour curfew on a dozen neighborhoods in a northeastern city that is a stronghold of the armed group Boko Haram. Residents of Maiduguri ordered to stay indoors as military launches strikes against armed group in the north.[98]

May 17, 2013 - Nigerian Joint Military Force deployed jets and helicopters to carry out air strikes on fighter camps in Borno. Airstrikes and shellings targeted at Boko Haram strongholds. 21 deaths reported.[99]

May 17, 2013 – Following report of civilian casualties in the military mission to dislodge Boko Haram insurgents, Human Rights Watch alleged the military was using extra-force to fish out Jihadists and the tactic directly affecting lives of civilians within vicinity of the insurgence. US Secretary of State John Kerry said he was "deeply concerned about the fighting in northeastern Nigeria" and urged the security forces to "apply disciplined use of force in all operations."[100]

Boko Haram has said it is fighting to create an Islamic state, but the group's demands have repeatedly shifted. The conflict is estimated to have cost 3,600 lives since 2009, including killings by the security forces.[101]

May 18, 2013 - 10 fighters were killed and another 65 arrested.[102]

May 21, 2013 - The Defense Ministry issued that statement that disclosed it had "secured the environs of New Marte, Hausari, Krenoa, Wulgo and Chikun Ngulalo after destroying all the terrorists' camps."
[103]

May 29, 2013 - Boko Haram's leader Abubakar Shekau said Nigerian military offensive is failing in its goal of crushing the four-year-old insurgency. In the video, he showed charred military vehicles and bodies dressed in military fatigues. Shekau called on Muslims from Iraq, Pakistan, Afghanistan, and Syria to join his jihad, he said in Arabic and Hausa.[104]

June 3, 2013 - US offers rewards for capture of African militants. About $27 million was offered for information leading to capture of African terrorist leaders. The highest reward of up to $7m is for information leading to the location of Boko Haram leader Abubakar Shekau. Smaller rewards were offered for any information that will lead to the whereabouts of figures in Al-Qaeda in the Islamic Maghreb (AQIM) and the Movement for Unity and Jihad in West Africa. A reward of up to $5m was offered for veteran militant Mokhtar Belmokhtar. His Signed in Blood Battalion was held responsible for an attack on a gas plant in southeast Algeria in January in which at least 37 hostages, including three US citizens, were killed.[105]

June 5, 2013 – Boko Haram members flee to Niger (Nigeria's neighboring state) as Joint Military Task Force (JTF) arrests 55 terrorists in Yobe. [106]

July 5, 2013 – Boko Haram storms Federal Government Secondary School, Manudo, slashing throats of 29 students and English teacher Mohammed Musa. Farmer Malam Abdullahi found the bodies of two of his sons, a 10-year-old shot in the back as he apparently tried to run away, and a 12-year-old shot in the chest.[107]

July 7, 2013 – Gunmen suspected to be Boko Haram Islamists insurgents killed 42 people, mostly students, in an attack on a secondary school in restive Yobe state.[108]

July 9, 2013 – A Federal high court in Abuja led by Justice Bilikisu Aliyu sentenced four members of the Boko Haram sect to life imprisonment for the 2010 terrorism bombing in Suleija, Niger State. This becomes the first court verdict in a case of terrorism in Nigeria that has taken more than 3,600 lives. [109]

June 27, 2013 - Boko Haram Islamist sect member confessed to have killed 23 people in two days at Ngomari Airport Ward 'Bakin Borehole' area in Maiduguri, Borno State capital, His victims were a village head and police officers in the area.[110]

July 14, 2013 – Mass graves, tunnels and bunkers were found in Bulabulin Nganaram, Maiduguri, and Borno State capital. The Joint Task Force (JTF), spokesman Lt.-Col. Sagir Musa said that Boko Haram men who died in gun battle with security troops were buried in the graves. During the confrontation, some terrorists were killed in the firefight, including the main Amir of Bulabulin Nganaram (who was on the wanted list of the JTF with a ten million naira bounty. Many abducted women, girls, and children were rescued and handed over to their families by the Task Force. Decomposing corpses of those killed by the terrorists were also found in drainages and mass graves.[111]

July 16, 2013 - Defense Headquarters in Abuja disclosed that the ceasefire agreement signed between Federal Government and the Boko Haram sect had not been communicated about the ceasefire. [112]

July 19, 2013 - Gunmen attacked a police station and killed two officers in Kaura town, Kaduna State.[113]

July 20, 2013 - Three gunmen, suspected to be members of an unknown militant Islamist group, were killed by local residents in southern Kaduna, an area known as Fadan Kaje, close to Zonkwa in Zangon Kataf local government.[114]

July 29, 2013 - Army paraded 42-suspected members of Boko Haram sect arrested in their hideouts in Lagos and Ogun states. Some suspects confessed killing soldiers and civilians in the northern parts of the country. They also confessed fleeing Borno State to Western Nigeria as a result of Joint Military Task Force onslaught on the terror group in the Northeast and Central Nigeria.[115]

August 2, 2013 – "The Osama bin Laden of Northern Nigeria, Sheikh Abubakar Shekau, was reported to have been deposed by members of his own terrorist group, Boko Haram. Sources disclosed that the toppling of his leadership was a prelude to peace negotiations with the government of President Goodluck Jonathan. The group -- whose full name is *Jama'atu Ahlul Sunnah Lih Da'awa Wal Jihad* is said to have entered behind-closed doors negotiation with the Federal government for an elusive peace to the conflict that has claimed more than 3, 600 lives since 2009.[116]

August 4, 2013 - A clash between security agents and members of Boko Haram in the town of Bama sparked by an attack on a police base, lead to the death of one police officer and 17 Boko Haram terrorists. Another fighting in the town of Malam Fatori after Boko Haram attacked troops led to the death of two soldiers and 15 Boko Haram terrorists.[117]

August 6, 2013 - International Criminal Court (IOC) indicts Boko Haram for Crimes Against Humanity. In a report, "Situation in Nigeria," IOC says there are reasonably reasons that the violence and death of more than 3,600 people since July 2009, the group that aims to spread radical Islam in Northern Nigeria may have committed crime against humanity.[118]

August 11, 2013 - Suspected Islamist Militants, Boko Haram raided a Mosque in Konduga, Borno State - 44 Shot dead during prayers.[119]

August 13, 2013 - Boko Haram Leader Pokes Fun At US, France, Claims Sect Winning War Against Nigerian Military. Boko Haram leader, Abubakar Shekau in a released video claimed responsibility for the recent attacks in several Borno and Yobe communities including Malumfatori, Bama, Biu, Konduga, Gamboru Ngala, Gwoza, and Damaturu. About 100 people including 14 soldiers were killed in these attacks; the latest was August 12, 2013 attack in Konduga where about 44 people were shot dead when gunmen dressed in military uniform opened fire on worshippers in a mosque.[120]

August 14, 2013 - Nigerian Troops Kill Boko Haram Second In Command, Abu Saad. The Joint Military Task Force set up by the president to dislodge Boko Haram reported that the deputy leader of Boko Haram, Momodu Bama – aka Abu Saad was killed on August 4, 2013 during an onslaught on the sect on a Mobile Police Base and in Bama Town, Borno State.[121]

August 16, 2013 Another Islamic Sect in Northern Nigeria emerges as Boko Haram Threatens Kebbi. The sect, called 'Kalo-Kato,' and led by Abdulkadir Suwaba was discovered in Uregi-Kongoma and Kwana-Mariga districts of Rafi local government of the state. They were reported to be preaching "contaminated Islam," urging Muslims to disregard Hadith and the teachings of Prophet Muhammad.[122]

August 16, 2013 - Suspected Islamic militants have attacked a town in Damboa, 85km (52 miles) from the Borno state capital, Maiduguri, North-eastern Nigeria killing at least 11 people.[123]

August 19, 2013 - Abubakar Shekau, Boko Haram leader suspected to have died of gunshot wounds, the Military Joint Task Force set up by President Jonathan to dislodge the terror group announced that he was shut in Operation Restore Order. Mr. Shekau according to the Task Force "died of gunshot wounds received in an encounter with the JTF troops in one of their camps at Sambisa Forest on 30 June 2013" "Shekau, it disclosed was mortally wounded in the encounter, and was sneaked into Amitchide – a border community in Cameroun for treatment which he never recovered," The military said there was evidence Shekau might have been mortally wounded in a gun battle between July 25 and August 3 in the northeast, but the security forces were still seeking confirmation.[124]

August 19, 2013 - Boko Haram kills 35 and wounded 14 in Dumba village, Borno attack. [125]

August 22, 2013 - Suspected members of the Boko Haram attacked Gwoza and Gamboru-Ngala in Borno State killing 13 killed people in separate attacks in Borno. Gamboru-Ngala is a border town with Cameroun where only a bridge separates the two countries. Gwoza is about 200 kilometers south of Cameroon.[126]

August 25, 2013 - Boko Haram terrorists dressed as soldiers kill 14 vigilantes and wounded nine others in Bama, Borno State. The vigilante members were on guard duty when the sect members dressed in military camouflage came and lured them away with the information that they were needed at a meeting nearby. On their way to the meeting the vigilante members were attacked and killed."[127]

August 31, 2013 – About 54 people including 24 vigilante youths (Civilian JTF), 14 Shuwa Arab herdsmen and 16 civilians were killed by suspected Boko Haram terrorists in three different Local Government Areas of Monguno, Damboa and Nganzai in Borno state.[128]

September 6, 2013: About 50 people were killed in air strike on Boko Haram. The encounter with Military Troops of 5 Brigade of 7 Division, Nigerian Army, Monguno, and Borno led to the victory. The incident occurred when the terrorists laid ambush in two communities of Gajiram, the Headquarters of Nganzai and Bullabulin Ngaura of Konduga Local Government Areas of Borno state.[129]

September 8, 2013 – Christian Association of Nigeria (CAN) hails Nigeria President Goodluck Jonathan and the military Joint Task Force (JTF) for clamping down on the Boko Haram sect and reducing its attacks on innocent civilians in the North.[130]

September 16, 2013 - 18 Nigerian soldiers linked with Boko Haram gets death penalty and jail terms. Among the convicted were a lieutenant, a warrant officer and 16 others. The Military Court that found them guilty commenced hearing on their cases since July 1, 2013. The charges included offences such communicating with Boko Haram members, manslaughter and murder. The convicts were tried by the 3rd Armored Division under the jurisdiction or Area of Responsibility (AOR) the offences were committed.[131]

September 17, 2013 - 40 Soldiers Killed, 65 Missing In Fresh Boko Haram Ambush. 40 Nigerian soldiers were killed and 65 others were missing in a deadly ambush by suspected members of the extremist group, Boko Haram. The casualty, one of the heaviest for the military in its campaign against the militant group in Borno, Yobe and Adamawa states, took place along the Baga - Maiduguri road (the sect's stronghold in Borno State) on Friday, September 13, 2013.[132]

September 18, 2013 - 8 Nigerians killed as Boko Haram members in Army uniform attack Abuja legislative quarters. The Gunmen, all dressed in Nigeria Army camouflage engaged in a gun battle with State Security Service operatives at Gudu District of Abuja. 12 suspects were arrested by the security agents of the Department Of State Services (DSS).[133]

September 19, 2013 - 142 – the total count of bodies found at September 17, 2013 ambush and after Boko Haram's - Damaturu highway Massacre.[134]

September 25, 2013 – Boko Haram leader, Abubakar Shekau, reported killed by Nigeria Joint Military Task Force made an appearance in a You-Tube video indicting the military for claiming that he was killed during operation.[135]

September 26, 2013 - Boko Haram Islamists open fire in church, kill Pastor and his 2 children in Yobe. After setting fire to the building, the militants fled the scene.[136]

September 29, 2013 - Militants kill students in college attack. As many as 50 students were killed in the attack on Agricultural College in the rural village of Gujba, Potiskum, Yobe State, Nigeria.[137]

September 30, 2013 – Yobe Students Attack; College of Agriculture, Gujba, Yobe State students attack by Boko Haram rises to 78. The number, however, increased as more bodies were recovered from the bush. Gunmen wearing military camouflage with black bandanas round their heads went on rampage in Gujba community, opened fire on the students of the College of Agriculture, Gujba, at 3a.m. as they slept in their hostel. The gunmen also blocked the Damaturu-Maiduguri road and killed travelers. Many people were still missing after the attack.[138]

September 30, 2013 - Seven people were killed and beheaded in Makintamari village in Kaga Local Government in Borno state along the Damaturu/Maiduguri road. The beheaded according to eyewitnesses had their heads placed on their lifeless bodies on the main road. At the Makintafamari village, in a separate incident, gunmen also cut the throats of four persons on Saturday, September 28, 2013.[139]

October 4, 2013 - Military killed scores of Boko Haram in an air raid of the jihadist camp in Yobe. Fifteen members of the terror group were also arrested because of the raid. The launching of the air raid was a reprisal following the killing of 41 students and a lecturer at the School of Agriculture, Gujba, Yobe State.[140]

October 26, 2013 - In a gun-battle with suspected Boko Haram terrorists, the Nigeria Military killed 74 Boko Haram fighters on a raid in northeastern Borno state.[141]

October 29, 2013 – Boko Haram targeted military killing thirty- five. The incident occurred on Sunday, October 27, 2013. The bodies of the victims were brought to a morgue in Nigeria's restive northeast city of Damaturu, Yobe State. The attack is the first raid in a major urban center by Boko Haram in several weeks.[142]

November 3, 2013 - Boko Haram leader, Abubakar Shekau in a video circulated and aired on its website, Shekau claimed he led the October 24 attack in Damaturu in which 35 people found in military uniform were killed.[143]

November 3, 2013 - Gunmen kill over 30 people including the groom in an attack on wedding convoy. The incident occurred between Adamawa and Borno in Northern Nigeria. The attack happened on Saturday November 2, 2013 when the wedding convoy including friends and relatives of the bride and groom was making its way back to the state capital Maiduguri after the ceremony in Michika, in nearby Adamawa State. No group has claimed responsibility at the press time. However, Boko Haram (meaning *Western education is sacrilegious*) has claimed responsibilities in the past of such attacks. These attacks have peaked since the Joint Military Task Force and Nigeria security agencies launched an offensive to end an insurgency by Boko Haram Islamists in the North and Northeast Nigeria. [144]

November 4, 2013 – French News Agency (AFP) reported that 70 Boko Haram members stormed the town of Bama in Borno state on a convoy of motorcycles and pick-up trucks on Thursday October 31, 2013 and executed 40 people and razed 300 homes. Spokesperson in Bama local government area, Baba Shehu told reporters that 27 persons and injured 12. On a separate incident on Saturday, November 2, 2013, Shehu revealed that 13 people travelling on a bus in the same area were "ambushed by the (Islamist) militants and murdered in cold blood. [145]

November 9, 2013 - Two soldiers from a combined team of the Joint Military Task Force (JTF) and the Nigeria Directorate of State Security Services were killed in Kano during shootout with suspected Boko Haram members. Five members of the militant group were also killed during the 3-hour incident at Dan market quarters and Brigade.[146]

November 13, 2013 - 2 Nigerian groups added to U.S. list of terrorist organizations. Boko Haram and a splinter group, Ansaru, were named to the federal roster of terrorist groups after U.S. officials determined that they had received training and some financing from the Al Qaeda affiliate in North Africa. The designation of these groups makes it a crime for anybody or organization to materially and financially aid these terrorist organizations [147]

November 15, 2013 - Boko Haram *ThisDay* Bomber Jailed For Life. The terrorist behind the April 26, 2012 bombing of SOJ Plaza, Mustapha Umar, and a self-confessed Boko Haram was convicted of bombing the plaza and sentenced to life imprisonment. *ThisDay, The Moment* and *The Sun Newspapers*. The convict had driven a Honda

Academy car with explosives and denoted the devices. Three persons were killed and many injured, while property estimated in millions of Naira destroyed.[148]

November 17, 2013 - [A] French priest working in northern Cameroon in an area where Boko Haram is known to operate. No one has yet claimed responsibility.[149]

November 18, 2013 – A 63-year old French citizen, Francis Collomp abducted by Islamic militants in the Northern city of Zaria since December 19, 2012 escaped from his kidnappers. According to Police report, he escaped while his captors were praying. He was met on arrival in France by the French Prime Minister and his (Collomp's) relatives.[149]

November 19, 2013 – Joint Military Task Force conducted a raid in Kano to flush out militants – Boko Haram members using a private building in a commercial center to conduct its terror attacks in Gayawa village, Ungogo Local Government area of Kano state. There were reported multiple explosions and sporadic gunshots. The raid lasted for hours and there were fears of heavy casualties among the suspected insurgents. The raid came as an aftermath of terror attacks on November 9, 2013 that left two soldiers and two suspected terrorists killed in the city. [150]

November 20, 2013 – Five suspected Boko Haram members were paraded before journalists for allegedly planning a deadly attack on Igala,

Kogi State. One of the suspects is Kogi State University Assistant Professor of Arabic and Islamic Studies, Dr. Mohammed Nazeef Yunus. He was identified as the spiritual leader and coordinator for Boko Haram in the state. [151]

November 25, 2013 – International Criminal Court has ruled the confrontation between the Nigeria government (Joint Military Task Force) and terrorist group Boko Haram as a "Civil War." Office of the Prosecutor (OTP) of the ICC in its official declaration disclosed that the conflict qualified as an armed conflict of non-international character. In accordance with Geneva Conventions, a "Non-International Armed Conflict" (NIAC) is the technical name for a civil war OPT indicated that similar manner that the resolution by the International Committee for the Red Cross (ICRC) was made in 2013; it means by the standard of NIAC, the norms of international humanitarian law under the Geneva Conventions holds to Nigeria and is applicable in the conflict between Nigeria Joint Military Task Force and Boko Haram. [152]

December 2, 2013 – Boko Haram raided Air Force Base very close to Maiduguri International Airport. No reports of causalities but the International Airport were closed by the Joint Military Task Force, set up by the Federal Government to quell the insurgent. [153]

December 20, 2013. The mastermind of deadly Christmas day bombing of St Theresa Catholic Church that killed 44 people in 2011, Kabiru Sokoto sentenced to life imprisonment. According to his personal testimony during his trial, he belonged to Boko Haram's Shura Council of Islamist sect. [154]

December 20, 2013 - Boko Haram on early morning hours (3.a.m in the morning – Nigeria's time) attacked the 202 Army Battalion Barracks in Bama. Media report disclosed that insurgents attacked with heavy arms and ammunition. The fight according to the report lasted until 7.a.m in the morning and left several women and children of soldiers in the Barracks dead.[15]

December 24, 2013 - Nigeria's military disclosed it lost 15 members pf the armed forces during December 20, 2013 attack by the militant Boko Haram Islamic sect in Bama, Borno State. Director of Defense Information, Major General Chris Olukolade, said over 50 members of Boko Haram members were killed in the attack, and over 20 vehicles belonging to the terror group were destroyed during the combat to stop the attack by the insurgents in the Army Barracks.[156]

December 24, 2013 - Churches Cancel Christmas Night Services in Borno, and Yobe States as a precaution against Boko Haram's violence. Following security challenges, midnight masses were cancelled. The situation was said to be the same in military and police barracks, where activities were restricted. [157]

January 3, 2014 - A French priest, George Vandenbeusch, 42, kidnapped by Boko Haram was released. He was kidnapped on Nov. 13, 2013 when armed men broke into his church in North Cameroun and took him to neighboring village in Maiduguri where he was held. . He returned to France to the excitement of his family members who were present at the Villacoublay Military base, outskirt of Paris, along with French President Francois Hollade to receive him. [158]

January 26 & 27, 2014 - More than 70 people killed in the two separate attacks in a village and a market in northeast Nigeria. Boko Haram has continued its attack despite military strategy to end the conflict since military assaults on the terrorist group seems not to be working; Nigerians are calling for new strategy. This was after Boko Haram strikes yet again. [159]

January 29, 2014 - Catholic Bishop Stephen Dami Mamza of Yola Diocese in Adamawa State, Nigeria revealed Boko Haram's attack on out-of-station in Waga Chakawa on Sunday January 29, 2014 killed 31 Of His Parishioners and Injured 11.[160]

February 5, 2014 – After the January 14, 2014 Boko Haram suicide bombing attack in Maiduguri which 19 people were killed, President Goodluck Jonathan dismissed his service chiefs of the navy, military and air force and appointed new service chiefs. [161]

February 12, 2014 – Suspected Boko Haram members numbering in their hundred attacked a northeast Nigerian town of Konduga, Bornu State for hours, killing 39 people and razing a mosque and more than 1,000 homes. [162]

February 15, 2014 – About 400 men in the village of Bama left their village about 22 miles fled to Maiduguri, the Borno state capital. The villagers fled after warning from residents of Gombale village that

Boko Haram Islamists members had gathered in Gombale for planned attack on Bama. Boko Haram suspected that recruits - members of a vigilante group (or civilian JTF – Joint Task Force), were aligned and supporting the Nigerian army's fight to flush out members of the jihadist group out of the state. [163]

February 25, 2014 - Boko Haram killed 40 students. Residents of the town of Buni Yadi disclosed the attackers struck at night, slitting the throats of some students and shooting others at very close range .[164]

March 2, 2014 - 90 killed in two attacks in northern Nigeria. Twin car bombs exploded in a bustling marketplace in Maiduguri on March 2, killing more than 50 people. The victims were children dancing at a wedding celebration and people watching a soccer match at a cinema. In a Mainok village 60 kilometers (40 miles) away, suspected extremists also struck Saturday night, killing 39 people.[165]

March 4, 2014 - Amnesty International expressed shock at the increased attacks by Boko Haram in the North-East Nigeria. Nigeria Researcher for Amnesty International, Makmid Kamara disclosed that since the beginning of 2014 attacks by the jihadist had intensifies and over 600 people have been killed by gunmen, often suspected to be Boko Haram.[166]

March 14, 2014 - Suspected extremists attack northern Nigeria city, this time Military Barracks in the capital city of Maiduguri, the base of the Islamic terror group. The jihadists fought their way into the military barracks and freed several militants detained in cells at the barracks. Reports indicated that Boko Haram members released were shot as they attempted to es-cape from the military barracks. About 14 bodies of alleged extremists outside the barracks were found. Following military air and land, pursuit of the terrorist, many unaccountable home and innocent people were also killed.[167]

April 14, 2014 – A vehicle loaded with explosives blasted killing 75 people with 141 wounded. The explosion ripped through a busy bus stop at Nyanya Motor Park, about 16 kilometers (10 miles) from the city center the of the Federal Capital City Abuja. The explosives destroyed 16 luxury coaches and 24 minibuses. There were no claims for the bombing, however, all fingers point to Boko Haram, which has between January and March 2014 killed more than 1,500 mainly in the North and North Central Nigeria. The bombing marked the first time the Federal Capital witnessed any major bombing in 2014. Following the incident, Nigeria President was at the scene as he cancelled event scheduled outside the city. The bombing also came at a time the National Sovereign Conference put together by President Goodluck Jonathan was meeting in Abuja to tackle problems facing Nigeria and recommend ways forward to the country struggling with constitutional issues about rights of its citizens to coexist among its more 250 ethnic groups, embroiled in religious and political conflicts. Following the blast, the "National Conference" gathering at the Federal Capital Abuja immediately adjourned their sitting ostensibly over security concerns. [168]

April 13, 2014 – In Maiduguri, 60 people were reported killed by suspected Islamist militants in an attack on a village in northeast Nigeria. Another separate attack by the terrorist group killed eight people at a teacher training college in the remote village of Dikwa in Maidugri. Eyewitness account revealed after the attack in the midnight, Boko Haram insurgents retreated into the remote, hilly Gwoza area, bordering Cameroon – neighboring Nigeria country. [169]

April 14, 2014 – Armed Boko Haram members stormed Government Girls Secondary School in Chibok, Borno State at sundown and kidnapped more than 100 girls. The kidnap came barely hours after explosives had killed more than 75 people and 141 wounded - 16 kilometers from the capital city of Abuja. Boko Haram raided student dormitories after the insurgents opened fire on soldiers and police who were guarding the school. Since Boko Haram started its suicide bombings, military-styled assaults, a mass kidnapping targeting girls specifically is unprecedented in the group's rebellion since 2009.[170]

April 16, 2014 – About 121 Nigerian girls abducted by Boko Haram militants were reported rescued. 9 are still missing. One member of the terrorist group was captured according to military sources. As it appeared later, the story was declared not true[171]

April 30, 2014 - About 200 protesters marched through major streets in Abuja to the parliament demanding that an action be taken by the president and security agents to rescuer the girls.[172]

May 2, 2014 - Protesters surrounded Nigeria's parliament calling on the government to take more action to find more than 276 missing schoolgirls. They were kidnapped by Islamist militants [173]

May 3, 2014 – President Goodluck Jonathan ordered a probe into the abduction of more than 276 schoolgirls in the town of Chibok. The 2-member panel was to begin siting on May 6, 2014. Their mandates were to find out why the school the girls were kidnapped remained open while other schools were closed after recent attacks in the state. The panel according to the presidency will also ascertain the exact number of girls kidnapped and their identity. This is following incorrect figures released to the media about the actual number of girls kidnapped. Similarly, the principal of the school where the girls were abducted, Principal Asabe Kwambura disclosed, "Right now, we are going to publish the names and photographs of the missing girls so that henceforth there won't be any conflicting figures." [174]

May 4, 2014 - U.S. Secretary of State John Kerry revealed the U.S. would help Nigerian officials in their search for the 276 missing Nigerian schoolgirls kidnapped by Boko Haram. US. Top diplomat described the kidnapping of hundreds of children by Boko Haram as an unconscionable crime.[174]

May 4, 2014 – 20 days since more than 200 girls of Chibok Secondary school in Borno state, Nigeria were kidnapped by Boko Haram. About 10 dead bodies were found lying on a lonely road in Wala Village in Gwoza Local Government Area, about 130 km southwest of Maiduguri, the Borno capital. It was gathered 7 of the dead were between the ages of 15 and 17 years, of which 8 of them were virgins. [175]

May 5, 2014 – Boko Haram's leader Abubakar Shekau - speculated to have died from wounds sustained while pursued by the Joint Military

Task Force in Nigeria appeared on video tape. He admitted that his terrorist group abducted the girls. He warned that they were being kept as "slaves." The UK Guardian quoted from the statement on the video, "I abducted your girls," ----I will sell them in the market, by Allah. I will sell them off and marry them off. There is a market for selling humans. "Women are slaves. I want to reassure my Muslim brothers that Allah says slaves are permitted in Islam." [176]

May 6, 2014 - Boko Haram Abducted 8 More Girls in Nigeria, Police discloses. This incident occurred on Sunday night, May 4, 2014 in the village of Warabe, in Borno state. Eyewitness account revealed that the abducted girls between 12 and 15 years old. This new abduction came as the world was still pondering over the April 14, 2014 kidnapping of 276 schoolgirls. [177]

May 7, 2014 – United States sends technical support to assist Nigeria rescue the 276 kidnapped schoolgirls. This was after U.S. Secretary of State U.S. Secretary of State John Kerry called the abductions an "unconscionable crime," and pledged to aid the Nigerian government in its hunt for the kidnappers. He remarked, "We will do everything possible to support the Nigerian government to return these young women to their homes and hold the perpetrators to justice. [178]

May 9, 2014 – Technical experts from the United States, Britain and China arrive Nigeria to assist in the rescue effort of the 276 abducted Government Secondary School Chibok even as intelligence reports indicated that the girls may have been slit into smaller groups and taken across bordering countries of Chad and Cameroon. [179]

May 10, 2014 - First Lady, Michelle Obama took over the president's weekly radio and Internet address – as United States celebrates Mothers' Day to address the April 14, 2014 abduction of the Chibok schoolgirls from their dormitory. She remarked that what happened in Nigeria is not an isolated incident, the first lady said, but is "a story we see every day as girls around the world risk their lives to pursue their ambitions."[180]

May 12, 2014 - Boko Haram released new video where its leader, Abubakar Shekua showed about 100 missing Nigerian schoolgirls. He alleged the girls have converted to Islam, and would be released in exchange for Boko Haram militant prisoners held by the Nigerian authorities. The girls who Shekua claimed have been converted into Islam wore hijab and were reciting or praying in an undisclosed location. [181]

May 16, 2014 - A British – Nigerian born Aminu Sadiq Ogwuche was among suspects identified in the April 14, 2014, bomb blasts that ripped up busy bus station in Nigeria Federal Capital, Abuja killing more than 100 people. He masterminded the bomb attacks in Nigeria and fled to Sudan after the attack. Sadiq Ogwuche was radicalized at a Welsh university. Experts on global terrorism warn that his case may be the beginning of a new wave of British-Nigerian extremists moving across European and United States to fight for Boko Haram [182]

May 17, 2014 - Following Boko Haram abduction of 300 school girls at Government Secondary School, Chibok on April 14, 2014. The world rallied round in respond to rescue the girls. U.S., Britain, France, China and Israel sent in technical experts to assist Nigeria rescue the kidnapped girls. French President Hollande organized a summit of four West African countries – Nigeria, Chad, Cameroon and Benin in Paris. Termed "How to deal with Boko Haram", the conference held on May 17, 2014 for the first time termed Boko Haram, "Al-Qaeda of West Africa" and agreed to join forces to fight the globally connected terrorist network.

Chapter 6

Boko Haram – Negotiating Amnesty Amidst Spiraling Violence & Deaths.

When on July 29, 2009, the designated Boko Haram's leader Mohammed Yusuf died in police custody, his immediate successor Abubakar Shakur went underground for a while after escaping from the gun battle with security agents that led to the capture of Yusuf in his father-in-law's goat pen in Maiduguri. During the battle leading to the arrest of Mohammed Yusuf, more than 800 people were killed – the majority of them civilians. The death of Boko Haram's members in the clash was at least a success that the Nigeria security forces were quick to acknowledge. However, the victory did not stop, but rather intensified the spiraling violence committed in the North and Central states of Nigeria by the terror group.

Since the July 29, 2009 clash with security forces, Boko Haram has carried out a series of attacks including gun battles with security agents and suicide bombings of civilian targets. Its military and guerilla tactics included suicide bombings of Christians churches including ones located inside the Military Barracks, Motor Park and entertainment sports where mainly Igbos converge in large numbers. However, a majority of the attacks were carried out against members of the security forces. They included police stations, police check points, immigration, and prisons. Other targets were elementary schools, high schools, universities, newspaper offices, and the United

Nations building in Abuja that housed more than 26 agencies of the international organization. Similarly, Boko Haram has attacked "infidels," and Muslims, their clerics, traditional leaders, and politicians from the North who criticized its ideology or tactics or was perceived to be collaborating with the state to identify and arrest its members. A handful of foreigners were also kidnapped, in particular in the months of January and July 2012.[1] Prior to these incidents, Boko Haram's leader had appeared in many videos posted on line claiming responsibility for the attacks and threatening future violence.

In total, more than 60 police stations and facilities in 10 Northern and Central States in Nigeria were attacked. Between June 7, 2011 and January 17, 2012, more than 142 Christians were killed inside church while they were worshiping. The attacks took place in 18 churches and were carried out by armed gunmen and suicide bombers across eight Northern and Central States. Between January 8 and September 2012, about 119 police (of the total of 211 officers) were killed by Boko Haram. In the same period, Boko Haram carried out more than 20 major attacks and 50 smaller assaults in the city of Kano state alone. These numbers represented, overall, the number of attacks by the jihadists in the country in 2010 and 2011 combined.[2]

A Boko Haram member told reporters that the Islamist group was on a revenge mission in retaliation for its members killed by security forces in the July 29, 2009 operation that led to clashes with the sect members.[3] Six members of the sect on trial for the November 2011 suicide bombing of a Catholic Church in Suleija, Nigeria States alluded to Boko Haram's sustained attacks and on-going suicide mission in Nigeria. One of the members of the sect told the court that they were avenging the death of its leader Yusuf at the hands of the security agents, [4] thus their attack on churches. Boko Haram's spokesperson, Abu Qada, remarked, "There will never be peace until our demands were met".[5]   The group's objectives include making Nigeria a failed State like Somalia, while imposing a strict Islamic culture on the entire Nigeria region ruled under fundamentalists' sharia laws to ensure that it can use the country as a base to reach Western targets in Europe and the United States. Boko Haram has carried these threats with attacks leading to deaths of more than 3,600 people, Nigerians and foreigners alike. While engaging in gun attacks and suicide bombings, its tactics also include kidnapping Christians, taking them to their camps, and forcing them to convert to Islam. Those that refused to convert have been strangled or shot in the back of their head.[6]

Even with a State of Emergency declared by the President of the Republic of Nigeria, Jonathan Goodluck, and a strong military deterrent offensive all geared to dislodge the group, Boko Haram insurgents have not been deterred from the attack of new targets. Motor parks where Igbos converge to board for road travel to the East have been targeted; buses carrying passengers mainly Christians travelling to Eastern Nigeria have been attacked at gas stations while stopped to fill gas. Other venues of attacks include police checking points, police stations, prison facilities where prisoners were freed and wardens shot to death; and immigration checkpoints, universities, elementary and high schools were attacked. Media houses and United Nations buildings were not exempted from attacks resulting in a high number of casualties.

Amidst the persistent attacks even as the Joint Military Task Force drafted more than 2000 military personnel to quell the insurgents following the Presidential State of Emergency declared on December 31, 2011 in three Northern States of Adamawa, Borno and Yobe, a cross section of Nigerians were still not pleased with the administration's efforts. As Boko Haram gets more sophisticated in averts the security agencies going after them, some accused the Joint Military Task Force as incompetent even though it comprised some of Nigeria's best military personnel; others believed that some renegades and supporters of Boko Haram within the military and the administration may be undermining the mission to route the sect out of existence.

Therefore, with the call for government to protect the lives of its citizens and put an end to the spiraling violence, the Presidency that initially was not opened to dialogue with Boko Haram seemed to be listening to the voices calling for amnesty for the members of the sect. The majority of the advocates for amnesty were Northern traditional and religious leaders. Nevertheless, the attention to amnesty did not stop President Jonathan Goodluck from suspending the constitutional guarantees of the 15 towns and cities in the North and Central Nigeria under the six-moth state of emergency. Still the State of Emergency did not ameliorate the security situation. According to Human Right Watch Report, "Boko Haram carried out more attacks and killed more people during the six months than all of 2010 and 2011 combined." [7]

Nigerians, having had enough, began to wonder if the difficulty in winning the battle against Boko Haram was as result of lack of equipment, military personnel training, or the mistrust of members of the security agencies especially as the President had alleged that some of his cabinet members and top politicians in his government sympathized or patronized the terror group. A statement to that effect was independently confirmed by the Chief of Army Staff (COAS), Lieutenant General Azubuike Ihejirika. He disclosed that some soldiers have been interacting with Boko Haram insurgents and divulging vital secrets of the army's military operations. [8]   While the Federal government admitted later in 2013 that the security agents were not trained to face the threats of terrorism like the ones unleashed by Boko Haram, the resilience of the group led to speculations that the composition of the group leadership, and its organizational structure, was more than the military could handle. Before Boko Haram emerged, Nigerians have accused their military of lacking in preparedness as they (military personnel) have become involved in politics and lacked focus. With Boko Haram, the fears that the military is facing gorilla-kind of warfare the military are not used to, makes the mistrust Nigerians have of their military experience to dislodge Boko Haram come true.

With links to Al-Qaeda in Middle East and in the Islamic Maghreb, majority of Nigerians feared that Nigeria might be heading to same unending terrorist attacks on civilian population by Al-Qaeda and its affiliates as witnessed in Afghanistan, Pakistan and Iraq. Even at that, evidence that the United States leading the Coalition Force in Afghanistan found it difficult to quell the insurgents with their sophisticated weaponry, money to fiancé the war and yet less successes; raises the fear that Nigeria may not survive Boko Haram's violence. However, security forces have overturned all these fears. They displayed tactical skills, determination and unrelenting efforts in their pursuit to dislodge the terrorists. The Joint Military Force set up by President Jonathan has achieved tremendous success, even though the security agents were accused of high-handedness and execution of Boko Haram suspects without trial.[9]

Therefore, the belief that Boko Haram is overrunning Nigeria security agencies and agents and winning in their war may not be true or false depending on what side a person belongs on the argument. That evidence exists that support that the repeated successful operation by Boko Haram members on its targets even with state of emergency and curfew declared in North and Central States in Nigeria was not in doubt. There is also evidence that supported the opinion that the military was not able to match the terrorist tactic and technique.

However, the overwhelming pursuit of Boko Haram and their fleeing their camps to escape to neighboring countries in Niger, Mali and Cameroon suggests victory. Similarly, the capture of many Boko Haram leaders and those killed support the argument that Nigeria security forces were making huge success on the war to dislodge the jihadists in North and Central states in Nigeria.

The news of the toppling of Boko Haram's leader Sheikh Abubakar Shekau, by Mohammad who assumed the leadership of the group in August 2013 was good news. The toppling of Shekau by Mohammed from organization with full name as *Jama'atu Ahlul Sunnah Lih Da'awa Wal Jihad*, meaning - "People Committed to the Propagation of the Prophet's Teachings and Jihad" was seen as a prelude to peace negotiations with the government of President Goodluck Jonathan by the group. The group, it was gathered have entered behind-closed doors negotiation with the Federal government for an elusive peace to the conflict that has claimed more than 12, 000 600 lives since 2009.[10]

While it is not clear how the peace negotiation will eventually work and be sustained, evidence of some captured ammunitions and documents found from Boko Haram's camps and hideouts during raids by the Joint Military Task Force confirmed that the group has international affiliations. Identities of non-Nigerians were also found at camps and building used by Boko Haram for its operations in Maiduguri. Pundits also believed that Boko Haram has evolved into factions not just the known one – Ansaru. In essence, Boko Haram has advanced into cell-based organizations that are unified under the control of its current leader, Shakur.[11] Therefore, it is not known which faction will lay down arms in case there is a negotiation and which of the cells that will continue attacks on its targets. This concern becomes more troubling amidst several underlying factors that may signal weakening sovereign state in Nigeria despite the intensify efforts by the Federal Government to dislodge or eradicate Boko Haram. Pundits have predicted without the Federal government addressing tactically economic, socio political, failing education standards, digital divide, and religious (using the same might and determination that it has pursued jihadist in addressing Nigeria's other problems, they (pundits) warned that it is a matter of time before another militant raises its head from any part of the country.

Meanwhile, the level of unemployment across Nigeria and, in particular, the North continues to skyrocket and does not help in the fight by the Federal government to capture insurgents and quell the violence. As a hungry man is an angry man, the poor witnessing their leaders living in extreme extravagance – in opulence while the majority of the people cannot afford a daily meal has its own downsides including security threats to the state. The situation does not help reduce violence as criminal gangs and political thugs soon joined in the menace.

These thugs and gangs – a majority of them unemployed youths, committed some of these attacks attributed to Boko Haram's spiraling violence. "Complicating the matter are criminal gangs in the north, including political thugs that are suspected of committing crimes under the guise of Boko Haram."[12] Coupled with poor governance and corruption in Nigeria, some of the critics of Boko Haram, even among Christians wished that the Boko Haram would target elites and political leaders rather than Christians or innocent people. This is in spite of Boko Haram's attacks shaking the citizens' psyche, the cord of multi-cultural and tribal relationships, and increasing tensions between the North (Muslims) and South (Christians).

These cross-sections of Nigerians wonder whether the government will be able to dislodge a cell-based and highly structured organization like the Boko Haram. Since the responsibilities of government to protect its citizens were fading and hope seemed lost; there were divided opinions as to the solution to the internal security problems posed by Boko Haram (with its affiliated terror group the Al-Qaeda). As Boko Haram insurgents were targeting Christians, innocent Nigerians, and foreign workers mainly working in construction sites, hospitals, and schools in the North, the desperation to put an end to the violence became the most pressing problem in every Nigerian's min.

In the North, the majority of the opinions represented in the media were of religious, traditional, and political leaders in the North. These leaders supported the granting of amnesty to Boko Haram members in exchange for a truce. The dominant opinion in the south, however, was the opposite. As majority of the victims – the targets of Boko Haram were Christians and Igbos from the Southeastern Nigeria, the voices from this region supported the arrest and immediate trial with death penalty for members of the terror group found guilty of the terror crimes that have taken more than 12, 000 lives.

However, amidst the divided opinions, the reality on the ground was that nothing seemed to be working. Boko Haram continues its viral attacks (even as July 31, 2013) taking lives in hundreds every month. Between the months of January and March 2014, it was reported that Boko Haram killed more than 1, 500 people[13] This was at the time the world was focused on Russian and Ukraine tensions where about 77 people were reported killed during the protest to ousted President Viktor F. Yanukovych.[14]

Although there was evidence that the Joint Military Task Force had done a marvelous job of pursuing and killing most members of Boko Haram, the use of the force to quell the insurgent seemed to not to be working. Where it worked, it attracted criticism from Human Rights organization, and the US government that condemned the accidental deaths of innocent people and the security agents' high-handedness of suspects and extra judicial killings.

Some in the North perceived the use of force to stop the violence as killing more citizens than the members of Boko Haram, international organizations such as the United Nations stressed that Nigeria's Joint Military Task Force against Boko Haram must thread with caution; observer human rights of citizen to stay away from unnecessary use of force and killings. Secretary General, Ban Ki-Moon, who was reacting to Boko Haram violence in Nigeria and the state of emergency declared by President Jonathan Goodluck, condemned the terrorists, but stressed the need for all concerned to fully respect human rights and safeguard the lives of Nigerians.[15]

Human Rights Watch and some US top officials, including the Secretary of State, Senator John Kerry, weighed in calling on Nigerians to guarantee that innocent lives were protected. They called for caution in the use of force by the security agents against Boko Haram. Since the security agents' treatment of detainees including Boko Haram suspects did not meet the International Standards as alleged by Human Rights organizations, evidence suggested that the human rights of suspects were not respected,

However, majority of Nigerians were less concerned about how Boko Haram members arrested by security agents were treated. Opinions held that the jihadists deserved no better treatment for killing innocent people in their private homes and in churches. Nigerians were more concerned with stopping Boko Haram's violence and sympathy for thousands of victims, majority of then incapacitated by these attacks for their rests of their life. They were often missed in this type of discourse, analysts disclose.

While these concerns were being raised, the precarious situation led to polarized opinions on what should be done next to protect lives of Nigerians under attack by Boko Haram. While some called for intensified military onslaught against the jihadists, others were calling for truce and amnesty. Divided with the South (Christians) against amnesty and the North (Muslims) - pro-amnesty, a variety of opinions predominated the news about what action should be taken next against members of the terror group to end its activities. Unfortunately, none presented viable lasting solution to the problem. Since January 29, 2009 Boko Haram had maimed and killed more than 10, 000 people (3, 600 killed and the rest seriously wounded and scarred with lifelong injuries), but it was not clear whether the United States interest and military presence in the region to eliminate the terror from Al-Qaeda in Maghreb (AQIM) was responsible for the Northern elders calling for amnesty for the terror group. The US located a Drone center in Niger (very close to Maiduguri) under the African Military Force – US/African Union security collaboration, but did not start operation until the jihadist in Mali took over the democratically elected government. Through French intervention, the insurgents were defeated, government was restored, but the jihadists fled to neighboring states including Nigeria.

Therefore, it was yet to be known whether the call from mainly the Northern leaders for truce and amnesty for Boko Haram was necessitated by the fears of displaced insurgents in Mali invading their territory to cause harm to the institution that these leaders relish so much, or whether the location of the Drone center within proximity of bordering states of Nigeria and Maiduguri in Northern Nigeria was also the reason for the expedited call for amnesty. What was clear was that Drone operations with their recorded casualties in Afghanistan and Pakistan were not attractive to the majority Northern leaders and some Nigerians as a tool to fight insurgents.

The reason that there was so much opposition to the use of Drones was that Northern elders were afraid of the reactions of their citizens when the Drones went into operation, and risked killing innocent citizens. Those worries were more than the fears and dangers posed by Boko Haram. However, as some claimed, Boko Haram, the displaced insurgents from Mali war and Libya insurgents after the fall of Moumar Gadhafi (some of the displaced jihadists) and the Drones – all threatened the institution of traditional and religious leaders in the North. Sources disclosed that these leaders did not want part of any of it. Furthermore, the use of drones threatens the internal security of Nigeria. The latter, even among Christians, is a reality that they do not want.

However, as witnessed from the testimony and media reporting, details of which the author included here, majority of the Amnesty advocates were Northerners. They included clerics, traditional and religious leaders as well as politicians. Some of the Southerners in the debate, who are in support of the amnesty, were people who in spite of being Christians had long business, social, and some other relationships with leaders in the North. As some critics highlighted, some of their views on their advocacy for granting amnesty to Boko Haram must be re-examined to determine the sincerity considering that only a few were talking about the victims of these attacks by the sect. Westerners including leaders of human rights groups such as Rev. Jesse Jackson, US Bureau of African Affairs' spokesperson, Ms. Hilary Renner, and Former US President Bill Clinton were among people calling for an end to the precarious security situation in Nigeria. He spoke at an award ceremony in Abeokuta, Ogun State Nigeria. He remarked that poverty eradication, education, equitable distribution of wealth and job creation programs for the teeming unemployed graduates in Nigeria could help minimize violence. He said that Nigeria would do better if her leaders efficiently managed her resources.

> "You have to somehow bring economic opportunity to the people who don't have it.....You have all these political problems — and now violence — that appear to be rooted in religious differences and all the rhetoric of the Boko Harams and others, but the truth is the poverty rate in the North is three times of what it is in Lagos. " [16]

The irony is that all the comments by the leaders were received with mix- feelings especially as the violence continues and nobody is sure whether amnesty will end the violence.

CHAPTER 7

Opinions on Granting Amnesty to Boko Haram Members - Views from Eminent Politicians, Traditional & Religious Leaders.

Is amnesty for Boko Haram fighters that have killed more than 12, 000 innocent Nigerians and foreigners worth any consideration now or in the future? Does amnesty for Jihadists that their objective is to Islamize Nigeria change the deadly attacks by a terror group that Al-Qaeda even condemned their tactics of beheading of school boys and kidnaping schoolgirls? Should terrorists who have shed blood by killing innocent people be allowed to go free? What about the victims of Boko Haram's inhuman acts? What messages will be sent to the world about terrorists that are granted amnesty while individuals they killed and their families are not compensated or see justice take it due course. These questions were at a point being considered by Federal government of Nigeria even President Jonathan tells that world and believes that terrorists could not be negotiated with for ny reason than it would empower them.

While Nigerians debated these questions, some Northern traditional, political, religious leaders were pressurizing President Jonathan to consider the option of granting terrorists amnesty and continue to witness the devastations therefore, Boko Haram is sustaining on the people and the nation. Some Nigerians, socially the opposition party to

President Jonathan's Peoples Democratic Party (PDP), question the reasons for bringing the idea up (even as the negotiations were alleged to be going on privately). People questioned, is the debate on whether the group should be granted an amnesty a distraction by the Federal security agencies while the Joint Military Task Force set up by the president mobilizes to attack the terrorist? Would the amnesty get the military prepared for military offensive that may finally disrupt attacks by Boko Haram terrorists and stop it from spontaneous suicide bombings and open confrontations with security agents? While none of the answers to these questions was forthcoming, there were divided opinions whether granting amnesty or federal authority using all within its means to either apprehend or kill members of the group should resolve Boko Haram terrorism that has global networks. Majority of Nigerians favor military offensive to stop the Jihadists from sporadic attacks on innocent people by whatever means or tactics the federal authorities devised to achieve that goal. However, majority of the people against military action preferred dialogue first with the terrorists. The voices supporting dialogue and eventual amnesty for Boko Haram fighters were mainly from North.

The Sultan of Sokoto, Alhaji Muhammad Sa'ad Abubakar, the traditional leader of Sokoto Emirate and the religious head of Muslims in Nigeria was among the prominent Northern leaders calling for amnesty for the members of Boko Haram. The leader of Muslims in Nigeria made the call at a *Jama'tu Nasril Islam* (JNI) council meeting in Kaduna where he urged President Goodluck Jonathan to consider granting amnesty to the dreaded Islamic terrorist group. He disclosed that the amnesty would encourage the Jihadists to lay down their arms.

In an apparent response to Sultan Sa'ad Abubakar's demand, President Jonathan, in the epicenter of Boko Haram deadly operations, openly rejected the call for amnesty to the insurgents.

In a town-hall meeting in Damaturu, Yobe State, Jonathan was blunt to the Islamic and political leaders, government functionaries, and stakeholders, telling them: "you cannot declare amnesty to ghosts. Boko Haram still operates like ghosts. So you can't talk about amnesty for Boko Haram now until you see the people you are discussing with."[1] He explained that amnesty for the Niger Delta militants was possible because the militants came out of hiding to meet in person with late President Umaru Yar'Adua in Aso Rock (laying down their arms). However, not so for Boko Haram Islamic sect as no leader of the group has showed up for dialogue.

The Catholic Bishop of Sokoto, Most Reverend Matthew Hassan Kukah in his Easter message to his parishioners and Nigerians called for amnesty for the Boko Haram. Reverend Kukah, who was a former Governor of Benue State in the Northern State of Nigeria, and also a former member of the Congress (House of Representative), remarked that "Many Christians have been tempted to use the persecution of Boko Haram, the destruction of Christian churches, and the brutal murders of fellow Nigerians as a justification for rejection of amnesty."[2] He disclosed, "Every true believer must understand that these sufferings, these trials are not outside the mind of God and His plans for our faith. The challenge is for us to remain faithful and steadfast so as not to be swayed by the dictates and exigencies of the moment."[3]

In an op ed. Easter message titled "Amnesty, Repentance, Forgiveness and Reconciliation," Rev Kukah also emphasized that persecution has been the hallmark of Christianity. International statistics data revealed that from the death of Christ more than 2000 years ago till date, some 70 million Christians have given their lives for Christ." "To reject amnesty is to place oneself at the same level as these miscreants. Their destruction on our country is not near the devastation of apartheid in South Africa. Yet, under President Mandela, Archbishop Tutu had to offer amnesty to leap frog the reconciliation process...The offer of amnesty will not solve all our problems, but it will bring us closer to a new dawn."[4]

Similarly, another respected clergy, the Catholic Bishop of Abuja, the capital city of Nigeria, Cardinal John Onaiyekan supported the call for amnesty. He remarked that it should be seen as a means of achieving peace in the North. He, however, said before the pardon should be considered, "members of the sect must seek repentance for the large number of person and property they have destroyed without any reason." Cardinal Onaiyekan in an Easter message noted that although the government had the power to give state pardon; it must be made with every caution. He remarked that Boko Hara fighters must seek forgiveness and repentance so that it would not look they did the right thing, and were persuaded to seek pardon from the state.

Cardinal Onaiyekan said, "as regards the case of an offer of amnesty to Boko Haram Jihadists, I understand that the security response in terms of arms, gadgets and trained personnel is helpful and necessary, but obviously not enough on its own. Government does well to reach out to all political forces and currents, so that the country can be on the same political page and jointly address this common menace, which   terrorism   is."[5]

Meanwhile, critics of these statements by Catholic leaders in support of prominent Northern leaders' call for amnesty for Boko terrorists were disappointed by these pleas when nobody was speaking for their victims. Opposition to the amnesty pleas was on the rise after statement credited to the Sultan. The Sultan who is the leader of the Jama'tu Nasril Islam (JNI) council – an Islamic religious organization that unites all Muslims in the country is a highly regarded individual whose words have relevance in all aspect of political and religious Islam. In essence, the weight of Sultan's statement is viewed as a consensus among Muslims in Nigeria. JNI is also regarded as the authority and forum through which policies that are political as well as religious emanate from Muslim leaders representing opinions of their followers in Nigeria.

Amidst the barrage of criticisms, majority of Nigerians decried the Sultan's request that President Goodluck Jonathan grant terrorist's amnesty, describing his plea for amnesty as unscrupulous. Chidi Eze, an Igbo from Southeastern Nigeria said that it is so unfortunate that Nigeria has become a place that anyone can kill, steal, and destroy and commit crimes against humanity and still get away with it. A leader of the pan-Yoruba socio-cultural group, Afenifere, Pa Reuben Fasonrati described the Sultan's call for amnesty as outrageous and highly unfortunate. He said, "I cannot imagine why a highly placed person in the caliber of Sultan should be seeking amnesty for Jihadists whose activities had rendered many people dead, others homeless and left thousands of children as orphans. "The sultan's call is obviously an indication that the caliphate is encouraging and condoning bloody violence...our position in Afenifere is that the Boko Haram members are evil. They should be identified and severely dealt with according to the laws of the land." [6]

Similarly, the Christian Association of Nigeria (CAN) rejected the proposal by the Sultan of Sokoto that members of the Boko Haram be offered amnesty. Speaking through its General Secretary, Dr. Musa Asake, CAN urged the Federal Government to rebuff the idea of any amnesty for the terror group. He wondered at the nature of amnesty the monarch was proposing for the terrorists. CAN, however, welcome the idea of Nigeria stakeholders to genuinely discuss the issues about Nigeria's development. It warned that for the talk about amnesty to hold water, the group must first renounce their extreme ideology and embrace the cease-fire plan. [7]

The Anglican Bishop of Wusasa Diocese, Bishop Buba Lamido, called for an overhaul of the CAN – the Christian body over its position on amnesty. In essence, he supported the granting of amnesty to Boko Haram fighters. His statement did not go well with CAN. The publicity secretary of the Christian Association of Nigeria (CAN) in the northern states, Elder Sunday Oibe responded to Bishop Lamido, and disclosed that there was no need for any amnesty for Boko Haram Jihadists who maimed and killed because they wanted to Islamize Nigeria.

While Bishop Lamido was reprimanding Christian Association of Nigeria (CAN) for insisting that President Jonathan grant amnesty to Boko Haram fighters, a newly installed Bishop of Akure Diocese Church of Nigeria, the Anglican Communion, Reverend Simeon Borokini, challenged the Jihadists to unmask themselves first before amnesty could be discussed. Borokini argued that as long as the group members are faceless, "it will be difficult for the Federal Government to grant amnesty to a faceless group." He, however, decried the level of insecurity brought about by terrorist attacks by group on Nigerians. The clergyman remarked that "The people should come out and show their faces as this would facilitate meaningful dialogue that anybody may want to have with them. "While regretting many lives lost as a result of attacks by Boko Haram terrorists, he asked the government to take a decisive action to stop the Jihadists from further killing of Nigerians.[8]

Bishop of Kubwa of Abuja Anglican Communion, Rt. Rev. Duke Akamisoko remarked if the granting of amnesty would bring a lasting solution to the security challenges plaguing the north, it is worth consideration. "While we are looking at how to solve the problem, the terminology, amnesty, is what I'm not comfortable with. If the government wants to speak with them to know their grievances, fine!" He continued, "I do not agree amnesty should be granted because of the level of destruction of lives and property terrorists have inflicted on the people and the nation. What about the Christians who were slaughtered by the sect? What about the churches destroyed or set ablaze?" [9] Akamisoko asked?

The Northern Christian Elders Forum (NOSCEF) announced that the decision to grant amnesty to Boko Haram fighters "is a call to other radical groups in Nigeria to rise up in arms against their fatherland, to be blessed when such an act should be treated as treason." Chairman of the group, Evangelist Matthew Owojaiye argued that intimidating the Federal Government to grant amnesty is the highest display of hypocrisy and lack of patriotism. He remarked, "Are such people not indirectly admitting that they are the shadows or ghosts behind the Boko Haram? We totally object to even discussing amnesty when nothing has been done for the victims of the Boko Haram."[10]

Former Vice President of Nigeria Atiku Abubakar under President Olusegun Obasanjo's administration between 1999 and 2007 was asked in an interview whether he would, as a president grant amnesty to Boko Haram. He said that if he was the President, he would not hesitate to throw the ball into the court of the Boko Haram leaders. "

> As was case with the Niger Delta militants, I would declare amnesty for the sect members with a deadline within which to surrender their arms. With the expiration of the deadline, if the sect members don't lay down their arms, then my government would be in a better position to face its critics that accuse it of not taking the initiative." [11]

Atiku Abubakar, who is also a founding member of the ruling People's Democratic Party (PDP), the party which the president is also a leader remarked, "The deadline for the surrender of arms would show whether the Boko Haram fighters want peace or not."

President Goodluck Jonathan in his Easter message to Nigerians reiterated that members of the Boko Haram sect were not Muslims, According to him, there is no true adherents of Islam that would subject the country to killings, bombings, and other gory attacks the way Boko Haram had done. He remarked that from the terrorists' modus operandi, the sect members were products of international terrorism network and not members of Islam or any other religion in Nigeria.

> "Those who mindlessly and indiscriminately attack worship places, schools, health workers, motor-parks, banks and ordinary road users must be seen as they truly are: the brainwashed pawns of international terrorism." [12]

He emphasized that the terrorists do not represent any true religion or section of the country, and Nigerians must never play into their hands by succumbing to their nefarious ploys to incite religious, ethnic hatred and division among Christians and Muslims. He urged Nigerians to continue to exhibit restraint and understanding in the face of seeming provocations.

> "We must have peace, security and stability to effectively implement our agenda for national transformation in all parts of the country, and we shall continue to work ceaselessly to re-establish the prerequisite conditions for nationwide progress and development." [13]

He urged Nigerians to rededicate themselves to living in peace and oneness with all members of their communities, no matter their ethnicity, religious beliefs, or places of origin

Spokesperson of the US Bureau for African Affairs, Hilary Renner, disclosed the United States government is concerned about the on-going attacks against Nigeria's citizens, civil institutions, and infrastructure by Boko Haram insurgents. "The United States has already designated a number of Boko Haram's senior commanders as terrorists, shining a light on their horrific acts and cutting off their access to the US financial system.[14] She remarked that violent extremism requires more than just a security response. The group known as Boko Haram exploits legitimate northern grievances to attract recruits and public sympathy."[15]

Renowned American Civil Rights Activist, Rev. Jesse Jackson joined leaders that supported the Federal Government's decision to grant amnesty to Boko Haram fighters. On May 19, 2013, during an interview with journalists in Yenagoa, Nigeria, Jackson described the decision to negotiate amnesty with Boko Haram as a deliberate effort to end insecurity in the country. According to him, the amnesty offer must be open and honored, and implemented to include economic restitution. It must also include rebuilding churches and mosques and other structures destroyed by insurgents in Northern parts of the country. On the other hand, he remarked, within the United States, when there was civil unrest, there was a kind of state of emergency. "You can bargain and resolve the conflict in the North. You must have the ability to resolve conflict and not fight aggressively. It must not resolve into killing and being killed.[16]

The United States Secretary of State, Senator John Kerry also expressed concern about alleged human rights violations by Nigerian security forces fighting Boko Haram Jihadists. He raised the issue with President Goodluck Jonathan in an open discussion on May 25, 2013 when he sat beside President Jonathan at an African Union dinner in Ethiopia. His discussion on the security situation in Nigeria with President Jonathan publicly (in what international relations experts believed should have been a very private diplomatic dialogue) revealed the urgency and importance of the United States concerns. However, Senator Kerry defended Nigeria's right "to combat terrorism" but warned that Nigeria state security agents have to do so respect human rights." Prior to meeting with President Jonathan, Senator Kerry had also on May 17, 2013 took the unusual undiplomatic steps to publicly disclose that he "deeply concerned by credible allegations that Nigerian security forces are committing gross human rights violations, which, in turn, only escalate the violence and fuel extremism."[17]

Meanwhile, the former governor of Abia State, Orji Uzor Kalu joined in the amnesty debate for Boko Haram fighters. He renewed his calls for the amnesty. He disclosed that granting amnesty to the Jihadists is for the "best interest of Igbos." He remarked that when the Niger-Delta militants emerged and were bombing pipelines and kidnapping people, the Federal government was able to sit down and negotiate with the group. He pointed out that because of the amnesty, the Niger-Delta area is peaceful and the source of Nigeria's oil money is protected from destruction. He disclosed that Nigeria cannot pay a price in one area (meaning amnesty to Niger-Delta militant) and not pay price in another (Boko Haram).

Former Governor Orji Kalu, who was raised and schooled in the Muslim North, remarked, "Let Boko Haram leaders come out like the Niger-Delta militants did, and the moment they do, should be granted amnesty. If you can give amnesty to the militants you can also give to Boko Haram."[18] He revealed that he would be willing to be a mediator and negotiate with Boko Haram if he was asked to do so for "the benefit of peace in Nigeria; for the benefit of my Igbo brothers who are being killed all over…You can see that if anything happens in any part of the world against Muslims, Igbo shops will be burnt in Nigeria. This is not fair. It is not justifiable." [19]

He also remarked that he is calling on northern elders, northern Ulamas, and all the people to come together and stop Boko Haram's criminal behaviour. He disclosed the Islam that he knows is not criminality; Islam preaches peace and unity. He cited examples of how relationships between Muslims and Christians, Hausa and Igbos had traditionally been.

> "During the civil war, my father had a lot of houses in the north, and when he came back after the war, some people who were looking after his houses; they counted all the monthly rents from the time he left and gave it to him. I am not holding

forth for anybody but I am saying that is the quality of the good Muslim. So I believe that we should preach to our younger ones the values that we were known for."[20]

While the debate raged on whether the President Jonathan of Goodluck should grant amnesty to the terrorists, it was reported that on April 1, 2013 - Easter Sunday, the Jihadists ramped up their violent attacks in selected States in Northern Nigeria - particularly Kano, Bauchi and Borno State. Sources pointed to the continued talk of amnesty by stakeholders within the federal government of Nigeria as the principle cause for the increased level of attacks because the Jihadists capture on the division among leaders in Nigeria along ethnic and religious lines to remain steadfast in the fight to Islamize Nigeria. Precisely, the division among leaders on how to fight and combat Boko Haram has continued to send wrong messages to the Jihadists.

The Jihadists, it was leant launched a broad mass recruitment campaign in the Kano State and its environs. The recruitment exercise was reportedly headquartered inside the ancient Islamic communities of Kano metropolis. The new recruits were taken to the troubled West African country of Mali for training. The training, it was gathered lasted between 4 and 6 months. A majority of the new recruits arrived Mali by road transport.

Sources also revealed the leader of Boko Haram was a guest of a wealthy Islamic leader at a home located in the northern senatorial district of Bauchi State. The leader of the group had come to Bauchi to coordinate the Bauchi recruitment. They arrived in Bauchi two days before Easter Day on March 29 and according to security sources – departed to Mali on Easter Day. The recruitment exercise was reported to have netted the group more than 1,000 new members within 19 to

30 days of the recruitment exercise. Already the Jihadists have begun preparations for a Black June/July for the selected States in the Northern regions of Nigeria.[21]

With changing tactics and rising numbers of successful deadly attacks on the civilian population, police and military personnel casualties from ambush laid by Boko Haram fighters, the former Military Head of State of the Republic of Nigeria Major-Gen Muhammadu Buhari (rtd.), blamed insecurity in the country on the President Goodluck Jonathans administration. He Federal Government is poor handling of the economic and remarked that poor performance of the administration is the leading causes of political unrest in the country. General Buhari, who is also the leader of opposition party, Congress for Progressive Change told Hausa Radio Service of the British Broadcasting Corporation (BBC) in London that the problem of insecurity was not peculiar to the North alone, adding that there was no difference between the Boko Haram sect in the North and the militants in the South-South (referring to the Movement for the Emancipation of the Niger Delta (MEND) – the Niger Delta militants). According to him, "The world is very much concerned about two things - the problem of security and economic well-being of a nation. Security is number one. A country can only be economically viable if there is security. Nevertheless, how did all these crises start? How did the crises begin and assume this dimension?"[22]

He highlighted a connection between kidnapping and bombing. Buhari said that criminals abduct people and receive ransoms. He emphasized that "security is the responsibility of the state; they should know how these things came about."[23] Meanwhile, he urged President

Goodluck Jonathan to persuade Boko Haram fighters to accept dialogue as a means of ending spiraling violence in the North. General Buhari described the virulent sect, Boko Haram, as a creation of the present administration and urged the administration to stop blaming him (General Buhari) for the problem. He remarked that Boko Haram was a mark of failure of President Jonathan's administration.

In a response to the former head of State, the Minister of Information Mr. Labaran Maku said the amnesty being canvassed for Jihadists could only be considered when the group opens up for dialogue and negotiation. He maintained that amnesty could not be the first option when nobody from the sect has come out to discuss with the Federal Government. Mr. Maku explained that amnesty is usually an outcome of discussions and negotiations, whereby those being offered amnesty should accept the offer in principle with conditions attached. According to him, nowhere in the world has amnesty been offered unconditionally to a group that did not even come out to negotiate with the government. The Minister emphasized, "Amnesty could be part of the solution but can only come out of the process of dialogue and negotiations, but offering it unconditionally is not known.[24]

Maku warned that Nigerians should not over-politicize the issue. "People continue to compare it (Boko Haram) with the Movement for the Emancipation of the Niger Delta (MEND situation. We must not forget that amnesty for MEND came after a series of discussions and negotiations led by leaders of the Niger - Delta region and the combatants in the creeks."[25] He remarked it was after negotiations reached a certain point and there were commitments that the issue of amnesty was brought up. Amnesty, he remarked was not just offered without conditions and negotiation. Maku, therefore, urged politicians to see the issue of granting amnesty to Boko Haram as security and national issue. He warned that politicians seeking for votes in the oncoming election in 2015, and using such issues of national security not to unduly over-politicize this issue of amnesty. As the debate whether Boko Haram should be granted amnesty seemed to be dividing the country especially with the powerful political and traditional leaders weighing in with their opinions, President Goodluck Jonathan summoned a Security Council meeting with his chiefs of the Armed Forces Council. After the meeting, the president eventually decided to appoint a committee to look into whether the group should be granted amnesty. The amnesty according to the office of the president, one of the primary conditions for consideration of an amnesty was that insurgents must come out and show their faces before any negotiation for an amnesty will take place.

Former head of state and national leader of the Congress for Progressive Change (CPC), Gen. Muhammadu Buhari, former heads of state, Gen. Ibrahim Babangida, Gen. Abdulsalami Abubakar, the Sultan of Sokoto, Alhaji Sa'ad Abubakar, Catholic Bishop of Abuja, John Cardinal Onaiyekan and the leadership of the Northern Elders Forum (NEF) and other influential groups in the north (except the leadership of the Christian Association of Nigeria, CAN) welcomed the amnesty but the Jihadists rejected the offer.

Among North leaders who commended the president for setting up a committee to review the option to grant amnesty to Boko Haram was Hajia Turai Yar'adua, the widow of the former president of Nigeria, Umaru Musa Yar'adua. President Jonathan succeeded Yar'adua. Turai, urged President Goodluck Jonathan to forgive

Jihadists as her late husband did to former militants in the Niger Delta. She remarked that when Yar'adua saw that the people in the Niger Delta, particularly the children were dying callously, he (Yar'Adua) took it upon himself to grant amnesty to the militants to ensure lasting peace.

> "There is poverty in the North. What Yar'Adua did in the Niger Delta, let Jonathan do the same thing to the North… Let him sit down and think about the insecurity in the North."[26]

Turai Yar'adua also advocated youth empowerment, emphasizing that if the youth are inspired, the country would be empowered as well. Meanwhile, President Goodluck Jonathan blamed leaders in the North (Muslims) for the continued Boko Haram violence. The President, made the remark at an event that he was represented by the Minister of Special Duties and Inter-Governmental Affairs, Kabiru Turaki. He categorically remarked that leaders in the Northern States in Nigeria have not done enough to unmask those behind the group's activities.[27]

The Christian Association of Nigeria (CAN) criticized the President for his decision to set up a committee that will pave the way for amnesty for the Boko Haram Islamic sect. The Public Relations Officer of CAN (Northern states and Abuja), Mr. Sunny Oibe said,

> "If the government has decided to set up a committee to consider granting amnesty to Boko Haram under the watchful eyes of the National Security Adviser without compensating people that have been killed, it then shows that something is fundamentally wrong with our society and government.[28]

Mr. Oibe queried, how President Goodluck Jonathan said earlier he could not grant amnesty to ghosts not long ago, but all of a sudden decide to set up a committee for amnesty. He stressed during the time

President Jonathan was the Vice President to Umar Musa Yar'Adua, their administration did not go about chasing the Niger Delta militants; rather the citizens from the South-South region went and talked to the militants to lay down their arms and engage the government constructively.

Oibe emphasized the question is: who are the members of this Boko Haram? He warned that if the issue of amnesty for Boko Haram was not handled with caution, the decision would encourage insurgencies throughout the country to rise and destabilize the country.

> "It means that if you have to get government's attention, you have to engage in lawlessness. The granting of amnesty to Boko Haram goes to show that lawlessness is a profitable venture in Nigeria. It will encourage the younger generation to embark on lawlessness so that government will give them attention.[29]

Mr. Oibe explained that as Christians from the North who have suffered from inhuman acts as a result of Boko Haram's insurgence, the president must be ready to engage the Christians because the silence of the church does not mean that Christians don't know what to do.[30] He remarked that Boko Haram members is not fighting because of poverty, unemployment and hunger, rather, they are killing people because they wanted to create an Islamic state where extreme forms of sharia are their laws.

President Jonathan inaugurated a 26-member "Presidential Committee on Dialogue & Peaceful Resolution of Security Challenges in the North." Their main task was to look into whether to grant Boko Haram amnesty and under what conditions. Dr. Reuben Abati, the Presidential Media spokesman said President Jonathan in inaugurating the committee has urged its members to constructively look into the possibilities of engaging key members of Boko Haram, and define a comprehensive and workable framework for resolving the crisis of insecurity in the country. Alhaji Taminu Turaki, the Minister for Special Duties was nominated as the chairperson. The committee's terms of reference included developing a framework for the granting of amnesty; setting up of a structure through which disarmament could take place and the development of a comprehensive victims' support programme and mechanisms to address the underlying causes of insurgencies that will help to prevent future occurrences."[32].

While the presidential committee was to sit for the first time, Boko Haram from its Maiduguri headquarters issued a statement rejecting any plans to meet with members of the committee. It disclosed that the Shura Council, the highest decision-making organ of the Jihadists led by Imam Abubakar Ibn Shekau is the only person who has the power to in their sect to decide whether Boko Haram fighters will accept the offer of amnesty. Boko Haram warned, "We rejected any form of amnesty stating that we did not ask for it. [33]

Another faction of the dreaded Islamic sect, Boko Haram, has rejected completely any proposed amnesty for the sect before the even the Federal Government made the offer. Abu Dardam, a spokesperson for Boko Haram faction told the BBC in an interview that the sect does not respect the Nigerian constitution and is only guided by the Qur'an. Dardam said the sect does not recognize democracy either as a form of government or as any institution operating under the system.[34]

Meanwhile, Borno State Commissioner of Home Affairs Information and Culture, Mr. Hyeladi Inuwa Bwala responded quickly and appealed to Boko Haram members to see reason and embrace the offer. However, security sources warned of the implications of granting amnesty to Boko Haram whose leaders have refused any representation and dialogue. Inuwa Bwala remarked, "Even if you look beyond the fragmented group of the terrorists, what happens if tomorrow, all the almajiris and jobless street urchins troop out in their millions and say they are *Boko Haram* and they want amnesty, which of course goes with a package of allowances, rehabilitation and training, could the government afford the cost? Does the government have the resources to cater to them? [35]

It is therefore the implications of negotiating amnesty as a tradeoff to terrorism that worries many Nigerians and the precedent that this may likely set presently and in the future in dealing with terrorists. However, as witnessed since the Presidential Committee on Dialogue and Peaceful Resolutions of Security Challenges in the North was inaugurated, there seemed to be no negotiations even though the committee was working modalities for the amnesty. Claims of negotiation with the Boko Haram was confusing as there were claims and counter claims of such meeting, but not established is what faction was at meeting to negotiate amnesty. However, it was gathered than an unknown faction was actually negotiating for amnesty with the federal government. What was not also clear was whether the group was negotiating under the group that is controlled by Shekua, the known leader of the main Boko Haram or someone else's personal or group gains.

Meanwhile, the offensive against Boko Haram by the Joint Military Task Force continued. Boko Haram has not given up its counter attacks. This is as evidence with the July 29, 2013 revealed. On this day, Boko Haram simultaneously attacked enclaves in Sabon Gari, Northern city of Kano state. Jihadists attacked the motor park with improvised bombing pipes. The area is known as the business and social spaces for convergence of Igbos and Christians from Southeastern Nigeria. Overall, the Igbos have been the most affected ethnic groups by Boko Haram attacks in terms of lives lost and property destroyed. About 24 people were killed as a result of the attack. [36] On July 2014 in the same area of Sabon Gari was attack by suicide bomber that killed herself and 12 other people.

Overall, the Joint Military Task Force set up by President Jonathan was "gaining ground" in their offensive to dislodge Boko Haram. This was as news had it that Boko Haram splinter group has toppled Boko Haram's leader Abubakar Shekau. It was well-received news, but short-lived as the defiant Boko Haram leader emerged to announce that he was not dead. Shekau surfaced to make claims including the attacks in Abuja, Kaduna, and Lagos. He continued to show up regularly to broadcast his threats and determination not to release the kidnapped Chibok schoolgirls until the authorities set free his "soldiers," he claimed were captured and detained by the state security services.

When asked by reporters, whether the Presidential Committee on Dialogue and Peaceful Resolutions of Security Challenges in the North was justified since, the spiral of attacks by Boko Haram have not stopped rather increased, the chairman of the committee, Alhaji Taminu Turaki remarked," Is there a country in the world where the issue of terrorism has been resolved with the establishment of a committee....The issue of terrorism like the one in Nigeria, where we have many elements that are masquerading into it should not be resolved overnight. So it is something that has a lot of dimensions."[37]

Meanwhile, all the resources that the Federal government of Nigeria could gather, it has committed to dislodging Boko Haram. However, the Jihadists have successfully carried out multiple bomb blasts in Sabon Gari, where Igbos from Northeastern Nigeria reside, and have churches, shopping malls and entertainment parlors destroyed. These are spaces where people converge in large numbers. Boko Haram also carried out violent attack in Kaka and Kakawa Local Government Areas of Borno less than 24 hours apart of these incidents.

On the same July 31, 2013, fisherman and traders were attacked and their property destroyed when insurgents attacked their villages. These orchestrated attacks in spite of the military offensive by the security forces have led to capturing majority of the Boko Haram fighters and forced majority of the villagers on the border town of Nigeria with Chad and Cameroon others to flee to neighboring African countries. The pursuit of Boko Haram fighters into the forest has not lowered the anxiety Nigerians have of their safety. People are still afraid and not guaranteed of their security in locations in the North and Central Nigeria and beyond - where Boko Haram has targeted.

The Sultan of Sokoto, Alhaji Sa'ad Abubakar condemned the attacks in Sabon Gari and Borno State. In a statement, he said that Jama'tu Nasril Islam (JNI) was baffled by the act of unleashing terror on human lives which continues unabated despite visible number of security check points mounted throughout the North and Central States in Nigeria. The Sultan who is the leader of umbrella organization holding together all Muslims in Nigerian said that the organization received with bewilderment, the news of the orchestrated multiple bomb blasts in Sabon Gari resulting in collateral damages and loss of lives. The Sultan described the attacks as reprehensible, inhuman and ungodly. He sent condolences to the families of the bereaved, the Government of Borno and Kano States, Shehu of Borno and the Emir ofKano.

In a statement, the Sultan who is also Muslim religious leader remarked, "We once again call on all concerned as a matter of urgency to nip in the bud future re-occurrences, which we don't pray for. As it is becoming more and more glaring to the right thinking person, there is a grand design to push the entire North into deeper crises and by extension of the Nigerian federation, the Emir warned"[38] He called for calm and restraint by citizens to avoid plunging the nation into tribal and religious confrontations. With the report of the Presidential Committee on Dialogue and Peaceful Resolution of Security Challenges in the North ready but not officially available to the public, the Joint Military Force has shown no stopping in its campaign to dislodge Boko Haram, but at the same time, the precarious security situation witnessed in the country continues to rise.

While many Boko Haram's members have been captured or killed, there was no account of who is in charge of these splinter groups even when Boko Haram's leader, Abubakar Shekau was reported overthrown by a leader of another splinter group.   With Boko Haram's attacks still going on, following the same sporadic pattern of multiple bomb blasts - a symbol of Boko Haram Nigeria's - Al-Qaeda- style-operations, it is evident that the war on terror will not be won by military force alone. President Obama also reiterated during a town-hall meeting comments made in June 2013, while on a trip to South Africa. According to President Obama, the war on terror cannot be won by the use of military force alone. In essence, in a society where the people are deprived of their basic rights and needs and they are young and poor, the probability is high for persons facing these basic struggles to be persuaded by radicals to turn their back against the state. Rather than protect the sovereign state, they may likely be recruited, manipulated, and used to execute extremists' goals such as Boko Haram is espousing.

Therefore, the approach to resolving the problem of terrorism as international terrorism experts have warned is a holistic approach that is focused intelligence gathering and the use of force. The negotiation of amnesty for a terrorist group that have refused to show their faces or negotiate a truce is a wasted time and efforts, the experts revealed. Just as being poor or hungry does not make any person to rob a bank, the same as hunger should not or does not cause anybody to be a murder or a Jihadist. However, meeting the basic needs of the majority of the poor people may be one of the best motivations to stop Islamic radicalism.[39] An unemployed youth that is looking for job to meet his basic needs of food, water, and shelter could easily be enticed by promises by clerics or fundamentalists that meet these needs. The teenager may likely be persuaded to adopt extreme values of his mentor. When government and citizens ensure that young people, who make up more than 65 percent of the population of Nigeria are given jobs, the probability that the attraction to radicalism or crime would be drastically reduced.

In Northern Nigeria where the problem of unemployment is more pronounced and often by culture, people are prone to loyalty to elders or clerics – even without the largesse of providing these basic needs, any little incentive may probably win huge loyalty. When the teenagers are motivated with cash and other religious and material incentives such as free Islamic education, travels and cash offers in grants and scholarships, the indoctrination process becomes much easier to accomplish when the objective for these gifts is wrapped with religion.

When unemployed teenagers are lured with incentives and brainwashed, they believe that committing suicide bombing with rewards in paradise was the ultimate decisions for them. When the individual kills self to achieve the jihadists' goal of Islamization and getting rid of 'infidels,' he goes to paradise; this kind of indoctrination using religion to achieve the selfish goals of the Jihadists is not just very dangerous, but a serious threat to national security of Nigeria, the United States, The United Kingdom or elsewhere that terrorism is promoted.

Therefore, reducing the threats posed by Jihadists [like Boko Haram] needs a holistic approach from political, cultural, economic, social and ethnic perspectives. Since issues revolving around these factors could be used to create problems that would threaten the sovereignty of a nation, mixing these problems and adding religious a and ideological twits makes the matter a double tragedy for a nation. When these problems extremists exploit to motivate wannabe terrorists are not addressed by governments, political and religious leaders and other stakeholders including businesses and entrepreneurs giving jobs to young people, the likelihood that terror will be eliminated in Nigeria or elsewhere is not likely to happen. Today, it may be al-Qaeda type-terrorists; tomorrow, it may be either a mutated form of Islamic fundamentalists or Christian-conservative evangelists engaging in its form of crusade to establish bases in Nigeria or elsewhere. The world has witnessed these acts of violence in history; Boko Haram may not be the last of these fundamentalists groups as long as we allow the problems we should have taken care, and individuals that exploit them, including Nigeria youth's vulnerability to fester for that long.

CHAPTER 8

Nigeria -Shading the Image of a Failed State

Some of the root causes of the religious and sectarian violence in Nigeria may after all not have anything to do with religion, rather all to do Nigeria Constitution and the unresolved problems from the manner more than 250 tribes were forced to live together without plans to address difficulties emanating from the relationships. Therefore, understanding some of the real causes of so-called religious and political tensions in the country is an important step to finding solutions to these inherent problems destabilizes Nigeria. If these problems remain unresolved, pundits worry that the fragmentation of the country as a failed state as predicted is imminent.

However, others disagree - informing that Nigeria has overcome some of her most difficult political and religious problems, and survived them. Many others doubt whether the present violence in the name of terrorism by individuals or groups will predict better future for the country. General Don Idada Ikponwen is the former Provost Marshal of the Nigerian Army and is considered as one of the country's leaders. In an interview with Nigeria leading Newspaper, the *Vanguard* he remarked,

> "Let me say pointedly that it is no longer an issue for
> argument whether Nigeria has turned a terrorist state or
> not. Nigerian government does not promote terrorism as a
> policy, but Nigeria has become a terrorist enclave, where terrorists operate either on their own or in conjunction with

terrorists outside the region."[1]

General Ikponwen, an attorney and a security expert disclosed that Nigeria has become a terrorist state and as a result, citizens are losing their lives. "We are losing unquantifiable lives and properties, we are losing self-esteem, and we are losing our past glory to this perilous state of thriving terrorism in Nigeria."[2] He suggested for Nigeria to move forward, it must address the state of insecurity in the country. He explained that government and leadership at all levels must be seen as making concerted effort to create an environment where crime and terrorism will be unattractive.

General Ikponwen said, "Terrorism whether they are from the North or the East is terrorism. It is the use of violence to attempt to overwhelm the legitimate government to prove that a legitimate government is bad and inefficient to win the heart of the people. Terrorism is based on deep-rooted anger and disaffection."[3] He remarked that the primary purpose of government is to provide security and guarantee the welfare of the people. According to him, when government is perceived to be incapable of providing the security and guaranteeing the welfare of the people, the inevitable conclusion is that government is ineffective. He said, "Let me put it more succinctly; there is no government unless that government is efficient."

According to General Ikponwen the events happening in Nigeria, "the killings, robbery, murder, assassinations, kidnappings that flood the land, many of which the culprits are not traced or brought to book; with the way that stealing has become the order of the day, especially among highly placed individuals in government, when these people are not brought to book, when nothing serious is being done even to act as deterrence." He continued, " the way that people are amassing wealth and nobody is asking questions; the way that materialism has become the essence of life; the way that there is much vacuum in the system." Furthermore, he remarked, "the way that people find solutions to problems and nobody takes them seriously; the way that we create establishments and bring unserious people to run them; the way that we make government look as if it is there to serve the interest of those who are always friends of government, people who Nigerians call friends of any government in power; we as a nation have become a laughing stock, not only among Africans but the world at large. I believe that we cannot continue this way. The morale of well-meaning Nigerians is at its lowest."

World Christian and Muslim Leaders task Nigerians to Peaceful Co-exist

After days of deliberations by scholars from within and outside Nigeria on the situation in the country and what could be done to restore peace and order following Boko Haram repeated attacks and massacre of innocent people, the World Muslim League (WML) made a public statement. The group advised Nigerians to rekindle the once mutual understanding that existed among Nigerians irrespective of their religion, creed, and region.

The Boko Haram's violence also got the attention of the Vatican on Easter Sunday, May 31 2013. The new Catholic pontiff, Pope Francis in his Easter message - prayed for Nigeria. In his remarks, he said, "Let us remember in our prayers, those where great numbers of people, including children, are held hostage by terrorists groups"[4] This was an apparent reference to a French family kidnapped in Cameroon and believed held hostage in April 2013 by Boko Haram. The Pope called for peace among people of diverse religions and tribes. Among the hostages held at that period by Boko Haram was a French family of seven people, including the family head, Tanguy Moulin-Fournier. They were tourists and had visited a park in Northern Cameroon when they were abducted and brought to Nigeria by Boko Haram militants.[5] The hostages were later released. It was gathered the French government paid a ransom that the United States and some other Western countries have opposed the ransom as United State saw exchange of money for kidnaped Westerners as encouraging more terrorism that may be attracted by these incentives.

An Islamic group, Muslim Rights Concern (MURIC), supported amnesty for the dreaded Islamic sect, Boko Haram. The director of the group, Prof. Ishaq Akintola, said that amnesty was a viable solution to the sect's insurgency and terrorism. He remarked that such an initiative was needed to shield Nigeria from a second civil war, and possibly, a military coup. MURIC justified its support for amnesty because, according to the statement, it stands for peace, and gives life, hope and recovery.

On the continued hostility by insurgents, with rising daily death toll and insecurity all over North and Central states in Nigeria, MURIC said. "Terrorists have one mindset, namely, to put asunder what government has put together, to destroy what government has built," it remarked. "Terrorists seek to create much havoc as possible in order to attract attention to their causes," MURIC concluded. The group reminded the anti-amnesty camp that there is a serious implication of a total rejection of amnesty. "This includes the possibility of escalation of violent attacks which may culminate in a second civil war with its dire consequences,"[6] it warned.

Boko Haram Terrorists – Impact on Relationships Among Tribes in Nigeria

Governor Rotimi Chibuike Amaechi of Rivers State, one of the state governors the Federal Republic of Nigeria with clean record of achievements. Despite his accomplishments, and being cast in doubt by opposition party in the muggy waters of politics in Nigeria, he remains one of the "action" governors and a credible leader in the country where these accolades are hard to come. In an interview, he remarked Nigerians have no guts for revolution. "Yes, revolution can happen outside Nigeria. However, here, I do not think so." He stressed, "Tell me what happened in Sudan, Libya, Zimbabwe, and other countries that have not happened here. Our elasticity has no limit. You do not pray for electricity to be regular but you know that some Nigerians pray 'God, let the light be stable today.' We pray without working to solve our problems and we think God will do what we are supposed to do for us."[7]

These statements were made at an event organized in Western part of Nigeria. Governor Amaechi is from Rivers State in the South-South Nigeria. Three days earlier before governor Amaechi's comments were made, a militant group, the Movement for the Emancipation of the Niger Delta (MEND) based in Nigeria South killed 12 Policemen in Bayelsa the home state of the president

Jonathan of Nigeria. Initially, there was no claim of responsibility for the crime, however, on April 8, 2013; MEND claimed its members carried out the attack on the police officers. Critics believed that the debate over amnesty for Boko Haram Jihadist might have motivated this particular attack. It was not immediately known the origin or tribes of the police officers killed, but many believed that MEND was equally seeking attention granted to Boko Haram during the debate and counter arguments about whether Boko Haram fighters should be granted amnesty or not.

CNK news editorial commentary asked, "Bravery" in killing our Policemen….would the president be granting Niger Delta Militants amnesty just as he planned to grant Boko Haram?" From the comments, it may seem that there is no end to the violence in Nigeria, but the experiences from Nigeria's history showed that Nigeria like Governor Chibuike Amaechi, who is also perceived as an agent of social change is addressing what is truly Nigeria's character.

Multi-Religion, Multi- Problems – Boko Haram's Exploitation of Nigeria's Diversity

The United States is a very good example of a homogeneous society. Yes, homogeneity is a critical factor that sustains nations and even marriage between two individuals. When one talks of homogeneity, it should not be isolated to race or ethnicity alone. The so-called ethnic nationalities in America are too thin that the general American dream assimilates them. When you talk of homogeneity, you think of language, literacy, religion, directive principles, and values and of course ethnicity.

In the United States over 90% speak and understand English, about the same figure can transform their thoughts in writing, and an over whelming majority are Christians. This is homogeneity because birds of the same feather flock together. Nigeria is a nation with 50% Muslim and 50% Christians. The diversity could be exploited or harnessed for reasons that may develop the country or destroy the sovereignty of the nation. In the case of Boko Haram, the use of the same religion to divide people is what the terror group exploits when it targets Christians and their worshipping place to execute suicide bombings on the holiest of the seasons such as Easter Sunday and Christmas eve-bombing of Churches when the spaces are full of worshippers. The same as the attack of Motor Parks, residential and entertainment spaces areas where the Igbos reside or converge in large numbers. The suicide bombings at Sabon Gari bombing, and the attacks on passenger cars carrying Igbos traveling from North to Eastern Nigeria are signifiers of targeted assaults.

CHAPTER 9

Terrorism & Sectarian Violence - A Reflection on Nigeria' s Past, Present & Ways Forward

---

A critical look at Nigeria history reveals that the amalgamation of South and Northern protectorates – Christians and Muslims has led to ethnic and religious conflicts which groups such as Boko Haram capitalizes to propagate their ideology, and gain support in their jihad to Islamize Nigeria. Like the rise of fundamentalism in the North, Jihadists have use religion as undercover to express tribalism that shaped Nigeria's history including the leading causes of sectarian violence.

The origin of some of the events in Nigeria's history is attributed to relationships between the North and South on political and religious lines, the relationships of leaders and people within these frames. Moreover, how the Nigeria constitution interpreted these relationship. On another note, the relationship of the South (Christians) with the West by culture and religion - pre and post-colonial experiences is also part of the problem. However, the most identified and unresolved problems causing most of the sectarian and political problems in Nigerian remains the amalgamation of tribes and regions by the British without negotiated arrangement between people that being joined together.

Other problems destabilizing Nigeria included years of military dictatorship and its domination of power that some perceived was clueless to finding solutions to economic problems facing the country. With poor leadership of the ruling political class, and the masses [that were hopelessly intimidated and frustrated by directionless regimes], the neglect of the economy and in fractural growth were accumulated problems that contributed to building tensions that the present democratic administration inherited. The unfortunate development is Nigerians wanted quicker answers and solutions to their problems that took long time to accumulate. With people demanding quicker results, analysts identified lack of patience on the part of citizens as the frustration building up to undermine the little or major positive things government is doing to correct the mistakes of the past. However, critics disagreed, emphasizing the revenue Nigeria derives from oil export every month is enough to overcome Nigeria's problems or reduce them to the minimum.   Economists agree that average person on the street should feel the impact of government – if not directly on their lives with the wealth, she derives from export of petroleum products and gas. Nigerians they emphasized should have access to loans or capital apart from meeting their basic needs. Government, they emphasized must provide the foundation to make these things happen. It is this state of hopelessness that pushes people to seek leadership change, and election of politicians into office that ushers in economic prosperity.

The track of Nigeria's history reveals a porous national foundation with underlying unresolved ethnic and religious problems. These problems continue to affect peace, stability, and economic development of a nation with abundant human and natural resources to be one of the greatest economies of the world. Nigeria has the potentials of becoming the world economic power, but it will not be true until the economic growth reflects on lifestyle of the people.

On religious fundamentalism and impact on Nigeria's economic development, there is no doubt that the impact of terrorism could be enormous even as the violence is concentrated in North and North Central States in Nigeria. While economic activities in the South are active, there are goods and services that come from North that help to maintain Nigeria's economy. The disruption of flow of goods and services by Boko Haram terrorists is affecting Nigeria's economy. With the terrorists often capturing the photo opportunities on the media, the Jihadists are scaring away foreign investors. The media by making the voices of terrorists heard sends messages that disseminate their agenda of theocracy and fear that the Jihadists wanted to spread. The aftermath of these extremists' imposition of their views and agenda on the people is that they have no regard or respect for the opinions of a majority that hold different views from their extreme interpretation of sharia including moderate Muslims. They give no clue, cared less how their terror affects people's lives, investments and Nigeria's economy.

Leaders in Nigeria seem not to help to diffuse the extremists' religious views that violence arising from Jihadists does not just start overnight. No Nigerian leader, past and present will feign ignorance that he is not away that religious fundamentalism breeds in North and South Nigeria, with the Muslim extremists being the most violent. However, the same leaders that are aware of these deadly extremists in the North want to turn their attention elsewhere thinking that the problem posed by fundamentalists will go away. Some of them wanted to be politically correct by not interfering with religion until violence (as witnessed with Boo Haram) manifests on the streets and it becomes too late to prescribe a panacea that would have resolved the problem from the beginning when the extremists had little resources, power and influence.

Regrettably, in Nigeria religion and politics are inseparable entities. When leaders play politics with religion, it brings about intolerance and diversity in communication among the people is relegated to the back burner. When tolerance and diversity are not discussed as a key national development program, the lack of awareness that diversity communication is a huge sector that needs investment of time and money is part of Nigeria's problem. The result of lack of diversity programs is that divergent views and opinions are not tolerated and often dialogue that little sensitive would have maintained often fails and the anger from all sides not voicing their opinions escalate already tensed situation, thus the violence on streets as was witnessed in Nigeria during the cancellation of Miss World pageant in 2002. The fundamentalists hijacking of the rhetoric led to rioting and killing of 200 Nigerians. The pageant was eventually cancelled and moved to Britain. The fact that Nigeria is yet to come to terms with her past – psychological trauma of colonization by the British has seemingly left red eyes on Nigeria.

Nigerians history still affects events that spin the nation into controversies and often lead to escalation of violence, the loss of lives and property. When the subject is about religion, politics, the recall of past relationships among tribes brings in some people hostility to resort to violence, thus threatening the security of the nation. The mistrust among citizens also raises conspiracy theories, suspicion and controversies. These conspiracy theories, suspicions and controversies have defined and affected Nigerians and how they relate to one another.

The rise of Boko Haram and other fundamentalist groups in Nigeria have deep roots to Nigeria's history of religious extremists and their agenda of creating Islamic state or caliphate. As witnessed with Jihadists in Afghanistan, Iraq and now Syria, these groups metamorphose and as new ones form, the more deadly and technologically sophisticated they are. It is the reason why international community should not be treated in isolation what is happening in Nigeria with what is currently going on with Jihadists around the world.

With Nigeria and the fight against Jihadists, the past should be considered in shaping the future. Bok Haram in mounting their flag in a town in Maiduguri it captured and fully in control on August 23, 2014 is like ISIS in Iraq and Syria declaring their caliphate state. How the world reacts to these developments, will prediction the future – whether the global village is going back to 400 years history when Jihadist conquered and captured towns and cities in Middle East and Africa – and was heading to Europe but ended up in Turkey.

The loss of one of the opportunities to host Miss World pageant was in 2002. Due to fundamentalist's rioting 200 lives were lost and forced the event to be moved to London. The experience cannot be treated in isolation of Boko Haram's agenda of Islamization of Nigeria by introducing extreme forms of sharia in Nigeria. Bok Haram was founded in 2002. The birth of the terror group in 2002 and the rioting that saw the "parading of naked women" as against the Islamic sharia cannot be separated from the ideology that Western influence is sinful– which in Hausa language is what Boko Haram means. The coincidence touches on various historical facts to illuminate the circumstances surrounding Nigeria's short sightedness about the fundamentalists' agenda and how these radicals have played authorities. For authorities not to be aware of these brewing problems until they unleash terror is self-denial. The key question remains, why events that set Nigeria backward to Stone Age still repeat? These events have not only shaken Nigeria's history but tested the zeal of her people and the nation's interpretation of order, peace, unity and gravity as a stable nation.

Whatever lessons (if any) that Nigerians may learn from Boko Haram threats will shape her future. How Nigeria handles the Jihadists will influence Nigeria's history, and shape her future. Reflections about the past showed Nigeria has not experienced terrorism of any magnitude as Boko Haram. However, she can learn from the playbook on Iraq and Afghanistan to deal with the threats posed by Boko Haram. Since Nigeria is limited to how far it could wage the war against Boko Haram, the presence of the international community to assist provide logistics, intelligence and military assistance to rescue the Chibok kidnapped school girls is a welcome development.

As earlier postulated, the presence of the international experts on the campaign mission to rescue the Chibok schoolgirls should extend to fighting war on terror. This is as long as countries involved stay clear of the internal politics in Nigeria. Their role is crucial to the success of war against Boko Haram and terrorist in the West Africa region. Nigeria's stability is important to global political and economic stability. How Nigeria handles Boko Haram and try to correct its past mistakes will reveal her determination to be a regional power, but also a power to be reckoned with in global politics. Nigeria economy and innovative strengths on the rise may be limited by circumstances, how she deals with its past and its internal and external threats. Finding ways forward is only a decision Nigerians and their leaders must have to make.

Nigeria: Which Way Forward?

Nigeria could move forward if it protects herself from both internal and external threats that affect every aspect of her economy and the lives of people. On August 7, 1998, two massive bombs exploded outside of the U.S. embassies in Dar es Salaam, Tanzania, and Nairobi, Kenya, killing 224, including 12 Americans, and injuring 5,000. Nothing was known about the terrorist group operating in Nigeria; thus, responsibility for the attacks was quickly attributed to Al-Qaeda.

Less than four years later, Al-Qaeda operatives struck again, killing 15 in an Israeli-owned hotel near Mombasa, Kenya, simultaneously firing missiles at an Israeli passenger jet taking off from Mombasa's airport. The United States was startled by the attack, thus, the response to send a message that such assaults will not go unpunished. It was based in the conviction to take the fight to the terrorists' bases in Afghanistan and Iraq that ultimately led to the "War on Terror." On Nigeria's part, the country is yet to develop high-level intelligence surveillance system to monitor its enemies coming from across her borders in Africa and overseas to cause trouble in the name of Jihadists' movement or Muslim brotherhood.

After the September 11, 2001 destruction of the World Trade Center, it became obvious that Al-Qaeda's handwriting was on the walls of attack that brought down the World Trade Center. The United States decided to take the War on Terrorism beyond U.S. borders to

Iraq and Afghanistan. According to former U.S. Ambassador to Nigeria, Princeton Lyman, in a peer-reviewed article authored with J. Morrison on *Foreign Affairs* journal remarked that the Bush administration has designated the greater Horn of Africa a front-line region in its global war against terrorism and has worked on dismantling Al-Qaeda infrastructure there.   Lyman and Morrison explained the war on terror was going on, that the U.S. failed to recognize less visible terrorist threats in Africa:

> "Countering the rise of grass-roots extremism has been a central part of U.S. strategy in the Middle East, but the same has not generally been true for Africa"[1]

The authors also disclosed that Nigeria's Islamic challenge comes from a combination of religious, political, and economic factors. He remarked that Northern Nigeria with the Hausa-Fulani is primarily Muslim and has influential Muslim brotherhoods in Western Africa region and the Middle East. According to Lyman, after Nigeria's independence in 1960, Northerners dominated the political and military establishment. Throughout this period, however, the authors explained that Nigeria has retained a delicate balance between Muslims, and the mostly Christian population from the South. That balance is profoundly tested in the 21st century as a more fundamentalist brand of Islam asserts itself in key areas of the country.

> "This resurgence is partly the outcome of an internal debate which begun in the 1960 and fueled by religious scholars funded by Saudi Arabia – over the purity of Nigerian Islam. But an equally important factor is the changed political and economic fortunes of the north." [2]

With Nigeria's position in global affairs, the 2002 religious rioting that began when fundamentalists opposed to the idea of hosting of Miss World pageant, coincided with the time the U.S., under George W. Bush administration designated the Horn of Africa as a front-line region in his global war on terrorism. President Bush has worked to dismantle Al-Qaeda infrastructure in the continent. However, since the U.S. failed to recognize the presence of other less visible terrorists' threats in the continent, the existence of these less visible terror groups in Nigeria were responsible for the Miss World 2002 rioting that killed more than 200 Nigerians. That invisible terrorist group has since metamorphosed into Boko Haram and its splinter group such as *Jama'atu Ansarul Musilimina Fi Biladis Sudan* or "Vanguards for the Protection of Muslims in Black Africa".

Lyman and Morrison theses indicated that Nigeria intelligence should have been award of threats posed by Boko Haram for a very long time. In essence, for Nigeria leadership to feign ignorance on the root causes of terrorism in Nigeria is doubtful and unreasonable. Nigeria's leaders should also be aware that Nigeria is an emerging democracy that is gradually becoming regional and continental power. The authors warned Nigeria leaders to recognize that the country's stability requires addressing the unprecedented levels of poverty, and underdevelopment in the country – the major causes of conflict in the country.

While the Horn of Africa was designated as fragile nation where terrorists unleashed their terror; Nigeria leaders must be proactive with their strategies to arrest terrorists' assaults that project the image of a nation that has joined the league of unstable nations threatened by insurgents. They include Sudan, Eritrea, Ethiopia, Somalis,

Djibouti, Uganda, Tanzania, and Kenya.[3] Nigeria may be richer than most of these countries, but to eliminate terrorist threats not just in the Horn of Africa, but also in Nigeria. The United States. and European nations such as Germany, France, and the U.K. must join hands to address the continent's economic and political problems, not just with sending tactical and intelligence team to rescue the kidnapped Chibok schoolgirls in Nigeria. Reducing trade barriers and allowing more goods from Africa is one sure beginning to addressing problems in the continent. Direct investments by Western countries in some of the stable African nation are still very low.

As Ugandan President, Yoweri Museveni said during a White House visit on June 10, 2003, Africa does not need aid; they need the economic doors of the U.S. and Europe to unlock to African goods.[4] He emphasized "subsidies," cheap pricing of goods and services produced by farmers from the continent are few of the undermining factors that stifle Africa's economic development. He went further to show Africans work very hard, especially farmers, but due to underpricing, their products do not generate any income. In other words, his remarks were that Africa toils for Europe and the U.S.

As nature has a way of balancing acts, Museveni's statement should not be taken at face value because what goes around may come around, sometimes haunt us more over a long period time. The West and China may be benefiting from cheap labor and pricing of African products but along the way, we may pay heavy price for the poverty we created by neglect or isolating Africa. With such reasoning, we need to act now before it is too late. Africa must be recognized as part of the international community, leaders need proactive actions to market their countries' goods and services on the international market in exchange for hard currency that will provide revenues for other services including rehabilitation of manufacturing sector, infrastructure development, jobs and security.

Foreign aids and handouts do not sustain any economy in a short or long term. Trade, economic growth, and investments do. Presidential visits by U.S. and European leaders to Africa either are not enough. While it may give the president's views of Africa's problems, action is what matters and required most to see cash from in to the continent from other revenue –earning sources other than exports of minerals and natural resources. Africa must also not be treated in isolation as a destitute or a panhandler for foreign or international assistance to fight diseases and famine. She actually has resources from petroleum, gold, diamond, and precious stones, just to name a few, so she has many commodities to trade with the rest of the world.

Many African countries rank high among world producers of cash crops such as cocoa, coffee, and tea. As Museveni pointed out, poor pricing has denied Africa from benefiting financially from exports. Therefore, the impression that Africa must be granted aid (financial assistance) is ridiculous and must be dropped. Because, when media attention focuses on wars, diseases and disasters, the eyeballs of the world through media attention shifts attention from root causes of major African problems. On the raging wars that often frame Africa's image, the big question is who supplies these wars lords with arms when barely they have no money to feed few years (before they picked arms to fight), and suddenly they are in wealth and caring for large contingents of once, hungry, rag-tagged youth that suddenly turned into 'militias' or killing machines.

Listening to some of the media-talk shows and news commentators on the heights of the campaign on war on terror, orders were issued with video clips showing the military intercepting ships on the high seas of the Mediterranean and Pacific Ocean. This search for arms caches going to Al-Qaeda or other organizations designated by the U.S. State Department as terrorist groups is no doubt helpful in the campaign to ensure that weapons do not get into the hands of terrorists.

Regrettably for decades violence (military coup d'état, armed-uprisings, tribal warfare) reigned in parts of Africa - African warlords, previously addressed by some Western nations as "freedom fighters" have imported arms from Europe, Russia, China, and the U.S. without problems. Most weapons end up not necessarily in the hands of organized armies, but in the hands of child soldiers and fundamentalists. Even at the end of guerilla warfare (in some cases after civil war and after toppling of dictators such as in Libya), these arms remain unaccounted. Most of the weapons eventually find their way into the hands of bandits, allowing a repetitive circle of violence; taking more casualties than before.

The world may be witnessing the dismantling of terrorist networks, but with millions of arms floating in the open and black markets, not just in Africa, but in unsafe parts of the world, they provide easy instruments for terrorists and bandits to carry out, robbery, kidnapping, assaults, assassinations, street gang fights and wars. This violence affects not just Africans but people of different nationalities, their national interests, and the global community. When we live in an unprotected neighborhood, it affects directly or indirectly the value of our property and our quality of life in general.

Nigeria Joint Military Task Force against Boko Haram military raided a house in Barunde of Gombe in Northern Nigeria supposedly belonging to a member of Boko Haram on April 5, 2012. The security operatives seized 51 rocket launchers in a house used to manufacture rockets and improvised explosive devices (IEDs).[5] With these violence as witnessed in parts of Africa, there is no way any nation impacted by violence would sustain economic growth now and in the future.

Should security of Africa be left to Africans alone? While Africa accounts for 6 of the 10 countries with the fastest economies of the 21st century, these countries witnessing economic prosperity are changing the scope of their economic development; peace and stability remain the most important elements among others that have seen these countries develop. In essence, African nations require stability that brings about development. However, Africa still faces more challenges with the menace of terrorists than it has in its history. It is not just with Boko Haram in Nigeria, but fundamentalists across the continent in countries such as Eritrea, Ethiopia, Mali, Egypt, Libya, Tunisia, Algeria, Somalia, Djibouti, Uganda, Tanzania and Kenya.

With the connection of these Jihadists to their counterparts in Middle East and the oil money now available to the Jihadist groups in Iraq and Syria, there is need for a joint force of the African continent to reduce the menace of terrorists, now that some of them are becoming more dangerous than Al-Qaeda in Iraq and Afghanistan. The presence of international technical, security experts in Nigeria to rescue the Chibok missing schoolgirls is a positive development; however, fighting terrorism needs a complete focus, huge financial support and consistent timeless pursuit. In essence, fighting Boko Haram or any terrorists in Nigeria or Africa must be a sustained commitment by international community in support of countries experiencing this violence. It is important to also explain that the countries threatened by Jihadists must provide the leadership with international support.

Côte d'Ivoire fell into a political quagmire that destroyed all that former President Félix Houphouet-Boigny created for a country that used to be the model of Africa's democracy. Beautifully planned and maintained, it earned the nickname, the "Paris of Africa." It was a true example of what African countries ought to be politically. However, Cote d' Ivoire is yet to recover from war resulting from a presidential election mess that almost split the country into North and South, it was an example of an African nation that witnessed economic development through its own trade in its endowed natural resources. The world witnessed how the exploitation of tribal sentiments and the dichotomy almost led to Cote d'Ivoire almost becoming a failed state. Nigeria must learn from lessons of countries around the world that conflict and Jihadists have devastated that they may not recover any time soon or ever. Nigerians must therefore not allow their country be destroyed by forces that have nothing at stake or have interest of the country, rather have clandestinely worked toward their agenda of disintegrating the country.

In Europe and elsewhere around the world, nations are merging and combining resources as buffers to unstable domestic and global economies. At a time when nations are clamoring to create larger economic and political unions for strength and stability, Nigeria cannot afford to break apart. Years ago, it was unthinkable that Eastern bloc countries would ever join the European Union; today, it is a fact despite economic setbacks and financial meltdowns. However, merging nations do not just provide security but also economic advantages and global connections that are required for nations to stay alive in depreciating wealth around the world. Africa must embrace these economic and political realities of the 21st century in terms of economic and political collaborations and sharing common currencies.

In the absence of economic wealth, equitable distribution of wealth, poverty prevails; hence, Africa becomes fertile ground for recruitment by fundamentalists and extremists. In Africa, with more than 4,000 tribes, each group with its differences and idiosyncrasies, the expectation that desperation and tension caused by poverty would not lead to rioting, tribal/community clashes, killing and maiming would be foolhardy. In essence, it would be imaginable that peace will always prevail under these deplorable conditions. There is no doubt some use religion as a shield to steer hate and anger against their neighbors, others use the gun to start conflicts we witness around the world. Politicians want to win elections at all costs, including using character, verbal and physical assassination of opponents to have advantage over opponents

In Africa, where guns and ammunitions are easily available from all over the world at 'buy-one-get-one-free prices,' the attraction of prospective insurgents, terrorists and war lords is overwhelming, leading to these individual exploring war as viable option to achieve their selfish goals and exploiting the vulnerable – the youth of their country to achieving their selfish goals. Similarly, the more failed states in Africa, the more easy access to spaces (countries) for terrorists ejected from Middle East and African troubled states such as

Egypt, Somalia, Libya, Mali, are ready to invade and occupy new vulnerable countries. There are also some African countries not on the list of vulnerable or failed States, yet the fundamentalist clerics have made so much in roads into them with their spread of extreme forms of their religion. Some of the youths have been brain-watched by these clerics; others have been won over by promises of jobs and financial security to the unemployed among their recruits. In some parts of Africa, even where the government seems to be in charge of the sovereignty of the state, poor people (mainly youth) neglected by their governments have sought the mullahs and fundamentalists clerics as their only hope. This last group of recruits by fundamentalist makes the work of recruits by Jihadists much easier. The fear and what should be of concern to the global community is that some of the Jihadists' recruits are no longer children or youth from economic under-privileged class. The aborted attacks on board Northwest Airline's Flight 253, en route from Amsterdam to Detroit and the arrest of Umar Abdul Mutallab referred as the "Underwear-Bomber," highlighted the growing radicalization of children of rich people, not really born in Nigeria but with a Nigerian background.

The suspected terrorist in the Northwest Airline's flight helps to unravel the fears that experts on terrorism have expressed about the growing apostles of Osama Bin Ladin and their dispersion across the globe. Al-Qaeda in the Arabian Peninsula (AQAP) claimed to have organized the attack with Abdul Mutallab; they said they supplied him with a bomb and trained him.[3] It remains to be witnessed any counter government efforts in Nigeria or even in the West to reduce the recruits of the youth who often are brainwashed by their recruiters and not sooner they were recruited sow seeds of hate, which would-be terrorists easily imbibe, putting their lives in danger and killing the innocent in the name of religion.

Therefore, for peace to reign and global security to be guaranteed (which incidents around the world show it may have made it more difficult to accomplish, world leaders have responsibilities to address that harmful phenomenon. While there are several dimensions to addressing the unending problems, one aspect of achieving peace and security could be support of true democracy in these affected regions that Jihadists have over–run fragile governments. Another method of taking the youths out of unemployment is by investments by developed countries in regions that Western investments (not donations or foreign aids) have not reached. Long neglects and disregard to economic development of poor performing countries around the world including African nations should be a matter of concern to developed countries, the UN and world leaders.

When our neighborhood in a global village is affected by poverty and underdevelopment, no matter how rich or well we may assume we are doing, the reality is that our property values and our society's values are affected by these underdevelopments. It depreciates who we are as humans and as people and a nation. The IMF and the World Bank consist of non-governmental agencies positioned to address some of the economic problems facing developing countries because most of these countries, their leaders do not care about their people. It is in view of this observation that the leadership of these agencies that has been under the Western influence should also change. If the problems of the developing countries are to be addressed, it must be approached from the viewpoints of those that wear the shoes and know where it pinches most. Pundits believe that leadership from developing world that has experienced the problems these developing countries faced would be able to address these problems.

Similarly, they argue that since more developing countries are contributing almost 50% or more to world economy, the need for a leader of IMF and the World Bank that understands Africa's problems (or other developing nations) and how to address them would be the stepping-stone to resolving Africa's economic problems. As already witnessed since the 1960s, the "prescription" has not yielded the desired economic results. Therefore, a new paradigmatic approach is required in the 21st century in appointing an African or a leader from a developing country should always be in charge to direct the affairs of these institutions that have been identified as determinants of financial flow and development around the world better. It is an argument that some disagreed, pointing out that Western or developed nations offering these leaders have performed better job of managing resources.

Finally, since poor countries with huge natural resources need the expertise and the resources of advanced economies to advertise and promote their resources in the global market, the role of UN agencies, such as the World Trade Organization, World Bank and IMF should be to assist these nations harness their resources, through expert - technological and financial support to engage in more intensified promotion of entrepreneurship, manufacturing and trade. Nigeria is relevant to the geo-political and economic stability of the world. She cannot afford to be a failed state. It is the reason, majority of Nigerians are delighted with President Jonathan's decision to eventually invite the international community to rescue the Chibok's abducted schoolgirls and assist fight the Africa's front on the war on terrorism that is destroying a country that took the toil of founders of Nigeria and Nigerians to build. It is the anticipation that the international assistance to rescues the abducted Chibok Schoolgirls dis succeed. However, the mission should not end with rescue of the schoolgirls.

Terrorism is a network "business" not entirely about religion or ideologies as Jihadists have made us belief. This shifting paradigm of ideologies (business and religion) that international community must be concerned. It is urgent threat that needs attention to stop these insurgents wherever they emerged. Boko Haram declaring a captured Pulka village of Gwoza town in Maiduguri, Nigeria a Caliphate, barely two weeks after Islamic State of Iraq and Syria (ISIS) declared the areas it captured in Iraq and Syria Caliphate is not a mere coincidence. The ushering in "new era of international jihad" is a red flag to the global community that must not be taken for granted. It also revealed the suspected network between Boko Haram and its terrorist networks that has officially been limited to Al-Qaeda and Al-Shabaab. Al-Qaeda in Iraq and Syria were ordered immediately to pledge their allegiance to ISIS as soon as these cities in Iraq and Syria were captured and made a Caliphate.[6]

Boko Haram, Terrorism and the Global Community

Despite the deployment of more than 2000 military men and women under the Joint Military Task Force to dislodge Boko Haram after Nigeria President Goodluck Jonathan declared State of Emergency in three States in North and Central Nigeria, Boko Haram has continued to unleashed terror and killed thousands of Nigeria. With two or more factions, there is confusion as to who is in charge of Boko Haram as claims and counter claims continued to emerge as to who carried on what attacks. As could be witnessed, a sect of the terror group a week ago claimed that it toppled Shekau recognized by Nigeria and the United States government as the leader of the terror group.

As Mohammed who claimed that he was the new leader of the terror group disclosed, he coordinated the simultaneous bomb attack on Sabon Gari in Kano where 12 people died as a result of the attack, the Joint Military Task Force announced that Abubakar Shekau has been wounded and toppled, the Boko Haram under his command targeted many communities in the North and Central States where the group operated. Shekau has been declared a global terrorist by Washington, which has placed a $7-million (5.3-million-euro) bounty on his head.

In August 12, 2003, Shekau's Boko Haram recognized as the original group leader released a new video where he claimed responsibility for the attacks in several Borno and Yobe communities including Malumfatori, Bama, Biu, Konduga, Gamboru Ngala, Gwoza, and Damaturu. About 100 people, among them 14 soldiers were killed in these attacks. The latest was in Konduga, August 12, 2013 where 44 people were killed when gunmen dressed in military uniform opened gunfire on worshippers in a mosque.

Abubakar Shekau speaking in Hausa amidst intermittent victory laughter said the military lied about its victories over their sect. The video, received by journalists on Monday, shows leader Abubakar Shekau refute speculation that he might have been killed. "You have not killed Shekau," he said, saying that Boko Haram was responsible for several deadly attacks in recent months. Shekau – who is said to lead the group's most radical faction – boasted that his insurgents were stronger than the Nigerian military and that they were now strong enough to confront the US. "I'm challenging Obama," Shekau said, issuing similar challenges to French President Francois Hollande and Israeli Prime Minister Benjamin Netanyahu. "They are no match for me."[1]

"The military is lying to the world about the battle we had with them; they lied that they have killed our members, but we are the ones that have killed the soldiers." "We call on you all to repent and come to the ways of Allah. Forget about constitution and accept Shariah. We don't have socialism, we don't know communism, we don't want federalism, but we are Muslims. "You soldiers have claimed that you are powerful, that we have been defeated, that we are mad people; but how can a mad man successfully coordinate recent attacks in Gamboru, in Malumfatori, slaughter people in Biu, kill in Gwoza and in Bama where soldiers fled under our heavy fire power. We have killed countless soldiers and we are going to kill more. Our strength and firepower has surpassed that of Nigeria. Nigeria is no longer a big deal as far as we are concerned. We can now comfortably confront the United States of America.

"Let the world know that we have been enjoined by Allah to kill the unbelievers just like how we were enjoined to slaughter rams during Eidel Kabir. And we shall continue to kill those who strive to stand against the will of Allah by opposing Sharia. We don't mind if we die doing this because it is even a blessing for us to die in this cause and gain paradise. So we are winning on either side. So it is never too late for you to repent and join us on the path of righteousness," he said.[2]

The timeline of violence by Boko Haram indicated the huge impact on lives and the challenges it poses to the Joint Military Task Force and the people of Nigeria. With its objective to Islamize Nigeria, the jihadists "war" to make Nigeria a failed state is unrelenting. It is the pattern of Al-Qaeda in Middle East and its Somalia-linked Al-Qaeda in the Islamic Maghreb. Special thanks to the various media in Nigeria, United States and Europe for the attention to the despicable acts of violence by Boko Haram that have taken so many lives. I have cited your sources as authority to my credibility in bringing to the world the menace of Boko Haram; the harm to lives and families that have endured these attacks. Without media information to the public-, especially the Nigeria media that is less appreciated than they deserved, the list compiled here would not have been possible. Several academic and non-academic sources that I have not used until now, you provided opportunity to compare my list with what you have and update as I tallied the data you read now.

President Barack Obama highlighted the problem Boko Haram and other terror networks posed to the security of the global village. Nigeria is not alone and should not be seen in isolation in dealing with the problem of terrorism. As President Obama also highlighted in Soweto during a town- hall meeting with young Africans including youth leaders from Nigeria who joined the conference through satellite technology. "Terrorism is bound to exist in countries that have neglected or failed to take care of their people." He further revealed that the war on terror must be addressed by people in their respective countries where terrorists are based in as much as the international community must unite to fight the so-called war on terror.

The majority of the victims in all terror attacks are still citizens of the country where the terrorists are based. Boko Haram's majority 12, 000 victims are Nigerians. The same could be said of victims of terror in Iraq, Pakistan, Afghanistan, Indonesian, Philippines etc. The rhetoric is often "The West is the target of terror, but the majority of the victims are not Westerners." In fact, the bombing of the US Embassies in Kenya and Tanzania was the first of terror attack in Africa that was masterminded by Al-Qaeda in the Islamic Maghreb. Investigations to the attacks led to the Al-Qaeda involvement in the planning of the attacks. It also led to FBI declaration of Osama Bin Laden as the Most Wanted Person on its list of the criminals around the World. In these attacks, Africans were the majority of the victims even though Western institutions were targeted. Investigations later revealed that Al Qaeda undoubtedly carried out the bombing in response to American involvement in the extradition and alleged torture of four Egyptian Islamic Jihad (EIJ) members arrested in Albania two months before the explosion in Kenya and Tanzania took place. As was the simultaneous pattern of bombings – the trade mark of Al Qaida, the 1998 bombings of the U.S. Embassies in Nairobi and Dar es Salaam killed 224, including 212 Africans, 12 Americans, and injured more than 5,000.[3]

On the solution to the problem of fundamentalism and terrorism, there is no doubt that the military option or the use of force may not be the only solution to dislodging terrorism. It has more to do with the attitude of leaders, political and religious who exploit the weakness of the human mind and motivate the vulnerable weak to be motivated to certain ideologies espoused by religious or political bigots, most of the time for their (leaders') selfish interests. After examination of the suicide bombing that is used to "send" a message about the ideologies these radicals advocate, there is no single incident in all the suicide bombings or military-style attacks that these politicians and clerics in Iraq, Afghanistan, Pakistan, Indonesia, Philippines, Somalia, Nigeria or elsewhere have ever used their sons or daughters. Sending other children to die for the causes they espouse indicates that something is wrong, somewhere. The solution to dislodging terrorism is therefore the commitment of every citizen to fight the war. It entails vigilance; it entails ensuring that the so-called religious leaders and politicians that finance some of these groups must be exposed. Similarly, clerics that promote radicalism or extreme form of Islam that they have hijacked from the majority of good Muslims must be made to understand that they are wrong and in the minority. Finally, the statement by President Obama, that terror cannot be eradicated by military force resonates here. Indeed, the world should isolate regimes that treat their people as if they were skunks. The results is huge wealth of the country being siphoned through corruption and capital flight to overseas countries in Europe, United States, and now countries in the Middle East, Qatar and Dubai. These must be stopped. When terror happens, it affects us all.

A hungry man is an angry man; we can reduce the motivation by politicians and clerics to young and unemployed youths to join their crusade by sidetracking the lure by these fundamentalist-religious and political leaders who use their faith to lure the weak and the poor. When the world becomes a place where the majority of the youth are employed and have no reasons to depend on the clerics or politicians that drive to be motivated to terror, any kind of violence will be minimized. Like terrorism and racism, these like life are problems to be lived with, but we can reduce their consequences – now and in the future to save lives.

All Will Come to Pass...But at What Costs?

"...The Northern leaders must move very swiftly to find solution to the security challenges confronting the region. There have been too much talk, now is the time for action. Now is the time to call the people throwing bombs and grenades, and causing mayhem all over the region to order. Now is the time to summon an emergency meeting of the emirs and other traditional rulers in the region to identify the bad eggs in their communities and bring them to the table of discussion and negotiation, and if they will not turn a new leaf, turn them over to the law.

Now is the time to take advantage of the Jonathan administration's offer of amnesty and tell those opposed to peace in the region to embrace it or face the wrath of the community and the law of justice. Truth be told, if the region is on the boil, it is clearly a failure of leadership (in the region). No less. It is not every time we blame others for our woes. We also must look inwards, and take a slice of the knocks. If we all are determined and honest about the grave issue at hand, I am hopeful that all hope is not lost as we seek to navigate out of the Boko Haram quagmire..." -

Eric Osagie, Flipside, TheSun, April 29, 2013.

Acknowledgement

Special thanks and deep appreciation to Nigeria's national and international newspapers and magazines – online and off line dailies. My colleagues who communicated to me through mediated media. Also through daily newspaper news and articles that I was receive on daily basis. Thank you all. To my spouse, who is my encyclopedia, you have not only helped me review my words, but your knowledge of Nigeria and global events are exceptionally a blessing to me in my writing including this project.

I decided to go the length in citing sources of news stories and interviews to ensure that the international community that most times see the Nigeria and the Africa's problems from the perspectives of the Western media and International Press, could see Nigeria journalism and journalists that thrive everyday to inform the world through their excellent writing style, editorial positions and the power in objectivity they have; Nigeria journalists' audacity to face and challenges of status quo and defend the public from the butchery of elite club milking the people to death. I owe this book project put in a hurry to you and your group of talented reporters that I rate among the best in the world, considering the limitations you has unlike your counterparts in Europe and the United States. You have accomplished much and continue so with the little you have.

NOTES

1. Bush, George Walker." Britannica Concise Encyclopedia, (i) v 3.0. 2009: eLibrary (i). Web. 01 Oct. 2012.
2. The Guardian (2013, March 13) Retrieved July 12, 2013, from http:// www.guardian.co.uk/world/2013/mar/13/jorge-mario-bergoglio-pope-poverty.
3. President Obama at the dedication of the National September 11 Memorial and Museum on May 15, 2014. Retrieved May 15, 2014 from https://www.facebook. Com/White House? hc_location=timeline.

PROLOGUE

1. Africanspotlight.com (2013, September 21).Kenya President loses family members in Westgate mall attack that killed 39, injured 150. Retrieved September 21, 2013, from http://www.africanspotlight.com /2013/09/21/ kenya-president-loses-family-members-in-westgate-mall-attack-that-killed-39-injured-150/

2. Associated Press (2013, September 21). 39 dead in Kenya mall attack; hostages still held. Retrieved September 21, 2013, from http://news.yahoo.com/39-dead-kenya-mall-attack-hostages-still-held-212623649.html.

3. Human Rights Watch (2014, July 15). Nigeria: Boko Haram Kills 2,053 Civilians in 6 Months - Apparent Crimes Against Humanity.RetrievedJuly22, 2014 from http://www.hrw.org/news /2014/07/15/nigeria-boko-haram-kills-2053-civilians-6-months

4. Prosoccertalk.nbcsports.com (2014, June 1). Soccer pitch in Nigeria bombed, killing at least 40. Retrieved June 2, 2014 from http://prosoccertalk.nbcsports.com /2014/06/01 /soccer-pitch-in-nigeria-bombed-killing-at-least-40/?

5. Allen, J.L. (2013). The Catholic Church: What Everyone Needs to Know. Oxford University Press. New York. Associated Press (2012, February 17). "Underwear bomber Umar Farouk Abdul Mutallab sentenced to life in prison". Daily Mail (London). Retrieved August 18, 2013 from http://www. dailymail.co.uk /news/article-2102254/ Underwear-bomber-Umar- Farouk - Abdulmutallab-sentenced-life-prison.html.

6. New York Daily News (2011, September 27). Surface-to-air missiles looted from Libyan Army could end up in Al Qaeda hands, experts warn. Retrieved August 4, 2013 from http://www.nydailynews.com/news/world/surface-to-air-missiles-looted-libyan-army-al-qaeda-hands-experts-warn-article-1.955697. See also (2013, June 11). The Situation Room with Wolf Blitzer. Al-Qaeda Surface to Air Missile Manual discovered in Mali. (Cable broadcast). Washington, DC. Cable News Network (CNN).

1. BOKO HARAM – IN THE BEGINNING

2. *Punch* (2011, November 30). Al-Qaida wants to kidnap westerners in Nigeria. Retrieved June 15, 2013 from

http://www.punchng.com/index.php?option=com_k2&view=ite m&id=6188:al-qaeda-wants-to-kidnap-westerners-in-nigeria-%E2%80%93-report&Itemid=542. Algeria is also home to the AL Qaida in the Islamic Maghreb. The group identified by security agencies (European, US and African) as providing both logistics and training to the violent Islamic sect in the Northeast of Africa.

3. *The Nation* (2014, August 25). Boko Haram: Row over 'desertion' of 480 soldiers. Retrieved August 28, 2014 from http://thenationonlineng.net/new/boko-haram-row-over-desertion-of-480-soldiers/

4. *Premium Times* (2014 May 17). Boko Haram Has Killed Over 12,000 Nigerians, Plans To Take Over Country, Jonathan Says. Retrieved May 20, 2014 from http:// saharareporters.com/ news-page/boko-haram-has-killed-over-12000-nigerians-plans-take-over-country-jonathan-says-premium-t.

5. *African Spotlight* (2013, April 20). Boko Haram Freed French Hostages Recount their ordeal. Family members of French citizens were kidnapped in Cameroon on February 19, 2013; taken to neighboring Nigeria and on Thursday, April 18, they were handed over to Cameroonian authorities. See Also AfricanSpotloight.com (April 26, 2013). Boko Haram was paid N500 million before freeing French hostages – report. Retrieved August 4, 2013 from http://www.africanspotlight. com/tag/french-hostages/

6. Johnson, Toni (2013, August 31). "Backgrounder: Boko Haram". Council on Foreign Relations. Retrieved 2011- 09-01. Retrieved April 13, 2013 from http://www.cfr.org/africa/boko-haram/p25739.

7. Vanguard (2013, April 10). Boko Haram amnesty: You are on suicide mission, Christians tell FG. Retrieved April 11, 2013 fromhttp://www.vanguardngr.com/2013/04/boko-haram-amnesty-youre-on-suicide-mission-Christians-tell-fg.

8. CNN (2013, February 15). Attackers kill 3 North Korean physicians in Nigeria, official says. See also U.S. State Department Human Rights Report on Nigeria (2013). United States Department of State (2013). Bureau of Democracy, Human Rights and Labor Country Reports on Human Rights Practices for 2012. Retrieved November 21, 2013 from http://www.state.gov/j/drl/rls/hrrpt/humanrightsreport/index. htm?year =2012&dlid=204153.

9. Reuters (2012, January 9) "Islamist sect has support in Nigerian gov't: president." In September 2012, however, the military announced that they had arrested an immigration official and some security personnel alleged to have links to Boko Haram attacks in Borno and Yobe states. See "Nigerian security officers arrested for Boko Haram links,"

10. Vanguard (2012, January 9). Pres. Jonathan's bombshell - "Boko Haram members are in my Government!" Retrieved May 6, 2013 from http://www.vanguardngr. com/Pres-Jonathan's-bombshell- Boko- Haram-members- are –in- my-Government

11. Ibid

12. Ibid

13. AFP, September 29, 2012. The Nigerian authorities filed criminal charges in November 2011 against a senator from Borno State, Ali Ndume, for alleged links with the group, an allegation Boko Haram denied. See section below, Prosecution of Boko Haram Suspects. In February 2012, the authorities dismissed a police commissioner, Zakari Biu, for his alleged role in the escape from police custody of Kabiru Sokoto, the alleged mastermind of the Christmas Day 2011 bombing in Madalla. Vanguard (2012, February 27). Secretly Reinstated, Publicly Dis-missed. Retrieved March 26, 2013 from http://www.vang uardngr.com /2012/02/zakari-biu-secretly-reinstated-publicly-dismissed/

14. Punch (2013, April 3). Govt blasts Buhari for comment on in-security. Retrieved March 26, 2013 from http://www.punchng.com/news/govt-blasts-buhari-for-comment-on-insecurity/

15. Vanguard Newspaper (2013, April 3). Boko Haram Tactics Baffling _ Army Chief Alerts the Press. Retrieved April 3, 2013 from http://www.vanguardngr.com /2013/04/boko-harams-tactics-baffling-ihejirika/

16. Associated Press (2013, March 15). Head of US Africa command warns of Islamic threat. Retrieved June 10, 2013 from http://www.houstonchronicle.com/ news/politics/ article/Head-of-US-Africa-command-warns-of-Islamic-threat- 4357815.php.

17. Ibid

18. Boko Haram-Ansaru: We have killed 7 kidnapped captives. Retrieved March 17, 2013 from http://naijagists.com/boko-haram- ansaru-weve-killed-7-kidnapped-french-captives/.

19. Vanguard (2013, May 20). Rev. Jesse Jackson Backs Amnesty for Boko Haram. Retrieved, May 26, 2013. From http://www.vanguardngr.com /2013/05/ rev-jesse-jackson-backs-amnesty-for-boko-haram/

20. Ibid

21. Olusegun Obasanjo's second coming having ruled Nigeria before as a military head of state between 1976 and 1979.

22. BBC (2014, June 6). More Nigerian girls abducted by suspected Boko Haram militants. Retrieved June 10, 2014 from http://www.bbc.com/news/world-africa-27298614

23. American.Aljazeera.Com (2014, August 15). Boko Haram abducts nearly 100 boys and men during village raid. Retrieved August 28, 2014 from http://america.aljazeera.com/articles/2014/8/15/bokoharam-nigeriaabduction.html

24. Reuters (2014, June 8). Female suicide bomber hits Nigerian barracks: witnesses. Retrieved June 9, 2014 from http://news.yahoo.com/blast-kills-least-three-outside-nigerian-barracks-witnesses-144938127.html.

25. Black Lloyd, D. (1967). US Economic Aid to Africa. *African Studies Bulletin* Vol. VII, No. 1. March.

26. Susanne Rice (2005, June 27). US Foreign Assistance to Africa: Claims vs. Reality. Brookings Institute. Retrieved March 18, 2013 from http://www.brookings. edu/articles/2005/0627 africa_rice.aspx.

2. BOKO HARAM: THE REAL FINANCIERS - CASH FLOW AND ITS GLOBAL TERROR NETWORKS

1. Lyman, Princeton N. & Morrison, J. Stephen (2004). The Terrorist Threat in Africa. Foreign Affairs, January/February, 2004. Also online at http://www.foreign affairs.com/ articles/59534/princeton-n-lyman-and-j-stephen-morrison/the-terrorist-threat-in-africa. See also Jane Mayer, *The Bomb Dark Side*, Doubleday. See also Al Qaeda operative key to 1998

U.S. Embassy bombings killed in Somali. http://articles.Latimes .com /2011/jun/12/world/la-fg-embassy-bombings-20110612.

2. *AFP,* Washington (2013, June 3). U.S. Places $23 million Reward for Boko Haram Leaders, Shekau, 4 others. Retrieved June 30, 2013from http://vanguardngr.com /2013/ 06/ united-statesplaces-23m-reward-for-shekau-4-others/

3. Al-Arabiya News (2014, July 13). Boko Haram voices support for ISIS' Baghdadi. Retrieved July 17, 2014 from http://english.alarabiya.net/en/News/africa/ 2014/07/13/Boko-Haram-voices-support-for-ISIS-Baghdadi.html.

4. *The Nation* (2012, January 29). Tracking the Sect's Cash Flow. Retrieved June 29, 2013 from http:// www. the-nation-onlineng.net/tracking-the-sect's-cash-flow/.

5. *SundayTrust* (July 7, 2013). JTF Detains Borno ANPP Chairman. Retrieved August 12, 2013 form http://sundaytrust. com.ng/index php/top-stories/ 13636-jtf-detains-borno-anpp-chairman.

6. Ibid

7. Ibid

8. Ibid

9. Ibid

10. Ibid

11. Ibid

12. *SundayTrust* (2013, July 7). JTF Detains Borno ANPP Chairman. Retrieved August 3, 2013 from http://sundaytrust.com.ng/index.php/top-stories/13636-jtf-detains-borno-anpp-chairman.

13. *Tribune* (2013, February 13). Boko Haram's Funding Traced to UK, Saudi Arabia-Sect Planned to Turn Nigeria into Afghanistan.

14. Africvilla.com (2014, May 4). Funding of Terror Network: 'Boko Haram got over N11bn to kill and maim. Retrieved May5, 2014from http://africvilla. com/index.php/africa2/10-nigeria/2094-funding-of-terror-network-boko-haram-got-over-n11bn-to-kill-and-maim#sthash.CmuASV69.dpbs.

15. AllAfrica.Com (2012, February 14). Boko Haram's Funding Sources Uncovered. Retrieved June 28, 2013 from http://allafrica.com/stories/201202141 514.html

16. *Tribune* (2012, May 21). Boko Haram's Funding – Nigeria May Face International Sanctions. Retrieved March 19, 2013 from http://dailypost.com.ng/2012 /05/21/boko-haram-funding-nigeria-may-face-international-sanctions.

17. *Premium Times* (2014, May 12). Chibok Schoolgirls: Israel offers counter-terrorism experts for rescue mission. Retrieved July 6, 2014 from http://www. premiumtimesng.com/news/160555-chibok-schoolgirls-israel-offers-counter-terrorism-experts-rescue-mission.html.

3 BOKO HARAM – EXPLOITING THE ART OF MEDIA PUBLICITY AND PROPAGANDA

1. Boko Haram leader, Abubakar Shekau Message. You-Tube Video (2012, January 12) Retrieved September 12, 2012 from http://saharareporters.com/video/video-boko-haram-leader-imam-abubakar-shekau-message- President Jonathan.

2. ThisDay (2010, December 27). Jos Bombings –Group Claims Responsibility. Retrieved September 10, 2012 from http://allafrica.com/stories/201012280 145.html.

3. Leadership (2012, April 9). Easter Bombing - Bodies Were Lying Everywhere – Survivors. Retrieved on April 9, 2012 from http://allafrica.com/stories/ 201204090157.html.

4. Vanguard (2013, February 14). Nigeria: Boko Haram – Cease – Fire or Ceaseless Fire. Retrieved February 20, 2013 from http://allafrica.com/stories /20130216108/html. See also Sahara Reporters. (April 8, 2013). Dancing With Ghosts, Ignoring the Dead.

5. Human Rights Watch, October 2012. See also Imam Imam and Seriki Adinoyi, "Jos Bombings - Group Claims Responsibility," ThisDay (Lagos), December 27, 2010, http://www.thisdaylive.com/articles/jos-bombings-group-claims-responsibility/71232/).

6. Ibid

7. Human Rights Watch interviews with Christians in Maiduguri, Maiduguri, July 2010. See Human Rights Watch Report, October 2012.

8. Ibid.

9. Human Rights Watch Report (October 2012). Spiraling Violence.

10. Ibid.

11. *Sun News* (2013, May 26) Femi Fani-Kayode: The Woolwich killing and the Illuminati - More questions than answers - Some things just don't add. Retrieved May 27, 2013 from http://www. sunnewsonline.net/ news/femi-fanikay.

12. Ibid.

13. This is a part of conspiracy theory that was floating in colleges and universities and it was also used to motivate stu-

dents to be science inclined rather than majoring in arts and social sciences.

14. *Vanguard* (2013, April 3). Boko Haram insurgency, a conspiracy? (1). Retrieved May 26, 2013 from http://www. vanguardngr.com/2013/04/boko-haram-insurgency -a-conspiracy-1/

15. Ibid.

4 BOKO HARM TERROR ATTACKS – WHY IGBOS –

(SOUTH EAST CHRISTIANS) ARE EASY TARGETS OF

FUNDAMENTALISTS IN

NIGERIA

1. *The Daily Trust* (April 3, 2013). Agree on amnesty for Boko Haram and I'll lead negotiations - Former governor of Abia State, Orji Uzor Kalu. http://dailytrust .com.ng/index.php/politics/ 53813-agree-on-amnesty-for-boko-haram-and-i-ll-lead-negotiations. Orji-Kalu suggested that Igbos suffer most by President Jonathan refusing to grant amnesty to Boko Haram.

2. *AFP* (August 24, 2013). Thousands of Nigerian Muslims protest to demand return of Egypt's ousted President. http://www.africanspotlight .com/2013/08/24/thousands-of-nigerian-muslims-protest-to-demand- return-of-egypts-ousted-president/. Retrieved August 26, 2013.

3. *Associated Press* (February 19, 2013). French family of 7 kidnapped in Cameroon, including 4 children. http://www.foxnews.com/world/ 2013/02/19/7-french-citizens- kidnapped-in-cameroon-official-The five French

family members were kidnapped in border town of Nigeria and Cameroon as chips for exchange of Boko Haram members arrested and detained by the Federal agencies in Nigeria.

4. *The Sun* (April 20, 2013). Kalu tables issue of Igbo marginalization before British parliament. On line http://sunnewsonline.com/new/cover /kalu-tables-issue-of-igbo- marginalization-before- british-parliament/ Retrieved on April 23, 2013).

5. J.W.C. Pennington (1841). *A textbook on the Origins and History of the Colored People* (Hartford, CT: L. Skinner), 96.

6. Tudor Parfitt (2013). Black Jews in Africa and the Americas. Harvard University Press, Cambridge, Massachusetts, MA. 107.

7. George T. Bardin (1921). *Among the Igbos of Nigeria: An Account of the Curious and Interesting Habits, Customs and Beliefs of a Little Known African People, by One Who has Many Years Lived Among Them on Close & Intimate Terms.* (London: Seeley, Service & Co. 1938[1st ed. 1921]), 31-32.

8. Isichei, Elizabeth (1976). *A History of the Igbo People.* London, England: MacMillan.

9. [66] Olaudah Equiano (1789). The Interesting Narrative of the Life of Olaudah Equino or Gustavus the African.

10. Tudor Parfitt (2013). Black Jews in Africa and the Americas. Harvard University Press, Cambridge, Massachusetts, MA.

11. Blum. Jeffrey, D (1969, February 25). Who Cares About Biafra Anyway? Retrieved February 8, 2014 from http://www.thecrimson.com/article/1969/2/25/

who-cares-about-biafra-anyway-pithis/#.UvZKeb8r
Gew.facebook
12. Igbo Jews – Shavei Israel – For our Lost Brethren. Retrieved August 12, 2013 from http://www.shavei .org
/categories/ communities. See also Re - emerging: The
Jews of Nigeria. A Documentary Film by Jeff L. Lieber-
man. www.re.emergingfilm.com.

5. Boko Haram – Timeline of Terror Attacks in Nigeria

1. Mayer, J. (2008). *The Bomb Dark Side*, Doubleday Publish-
ing, New York, NY. See also Los *Angeles Times* (June 12,
2011). Al Qaeda operative key to 1998 U.S. Embassy
bombings killed in Somali. Retrieved August 12, 2012
from http://articles.latimes.com/2011/jun/12/ world/la-fg-
embassy-bombings-20110612.

2. *Associated Press* (March 15, 2013). Head of US Africa
command warns of Islamic threat. Retrieved May 12, 2013
from http://www.houston chronicle.com
/news/politics/article/ Head-of-US-Africa-command-warns-
of-Islamic-threat-4357815.php

3. *CNN* (February 18, 2013). Boko Haram offshoot claims responsibility in Nigeria kidnapping. Retrieved May 12, 2013
from http://www.cnn.com/2013/02/18/world/ africa/nigeria-
kidnappings/index.html

4. Bartollota, C. (2011). Terrorism in Nigeria: the Rise of
Boko Haram. *Journal of International Diplomacy & International Relations*. September 23, 2011. Retrieved June 15,

2012 from http://blogs.shu.edu/diplomacy /2011/09/ terror-ism-in-nigeria-the-rise-of-boko-haram/.

5. Boko Haram – Ansaru: We have killed 7 kidnapped cap-tives. Retrieved March 17, 2013 from http://naijagists .com/ boko-haram - Ansaru-weve-killed-7-kidnapped-french-captives/

6. *Vanguard* (July 16, 2013). Boko Haram ceasefire: Opera-tion continues until… – Army. Retrieved August 5, 2013 from http://www.vanguardngr.com /2013/07/boko-haram-ceasefire- operation-continues-until-army/

7. *Associated Press* (September 25, 2004). Clashes between security forces & Islamic militants leave 29 dead in Nige-ria. Retrieved February 12, 2012 from http://staugustine.com/stories/092504/wor_2602296.shtml. See also Human Rights Watch Report October, 2012.

8. Human Rights Watch Report October, 2012. See also *Associated Press* (October 9, 2004). Islamic militants kill three policemen, 12 abducted by Boko Haram in Northeast Nigeria.

9. Human Rights Watch Report (October 2012).

10. Ibid.

11. BBC News (July 29, 2009). Dozens killed in Nigeria clash-es. Retrieved June 13, 2011 from http://news.bbc. co .uk /2/hi/africa/8169359.stm.

12. *AFP* (July 26, 2009). See also Human Rights Watch Report (October, 2012).

13. *Daily Trust* (August 10, 2009). See also Allafrica.com (Au-gust 10, 2009). Over 100 killed in clashes in Nigeria city. http://www. Allafrica.com/stories/200908100881.htm.

14. *New York Times* (July 27, 2009). Scores Die as Fighters Battle Nigerian Police. Retrieved June 13, 2013 from http://www.nytimes.com/ 2009/07/28/ world/africa/28nigeria.html?

15. Human Rights Watch Report (October, 2012).

16. RTE News (July 27, 2009). Over 100 dead in Nigerian clashes. Retrieved July 20, 2013.

http://www.rte.ie/news/2009 /0727/120030-nigeria/. See also Human Rights Watch Report (October, 2012).

17. Human Rights Watch Report (October, 2012).

18. Ibid.

19. BBC News (July 29, 2009) Captives freed in Nigerian city. Retrieved January 10, 2010. http://news.bbc.co.uk /2/hi/africa/8174399.stm

20. Human Rights Watch Report (October, 2012).

21. Human Rights Watch Report (October, 2012). Also AFP (August 3, 2009). Islamist uprising kills 180 in one night – red cross.

22. Ibid. Also AFP (August 3, 2009). Police confirmed 55 killed in Bauchi, 45 in and around Potiskun, Yobe State and 4 in Wudil, Kano State.

23. *The Leadership* (September 8, 2010). Nigeria: Attack on Bauchi Prison - Boko Haram Frees 721 Inmates.Allafrica.com. Retrieved June 15, 2012. http://allafrica.com/stories/201009090034.html,

24. *This Day* (September 22, 2010). Boko Haram claims killings in Borno. Online at http://www.thisdaylive.com/articles/boko-haram/. Retrieved September 12, 2011).

25. *This Day* (December 27, 2010). Jos bombing – Group claims responsibility. http://www.allafrica,com/stories/20101228.0145.html. Retrieved September 8, 2012).

26. *Sunday Times* (January 1, 2012). Barracks bomb claims 4 on New Year's Eve. Retrieved June 10, 2013 from http://www.timeslive.co.za/sundaytimes/ article832114.ece/ Barracks-bomb-claims-4-on-New-Years-Eve.

27. *Tribune* (January 20, 2011). Boko Haram strikes again in Bornu, kills 4. Retrieved June 13, 2013 from http://www.tribune.com.ng/index.php/front-page-news/16402-boko-haram-strikes-again-in-Bornu -kills-4.

28. *Vanguard* (June 1, 2012) Nigeria: Kidnapped German, Six Gunmen Killed as JTF Invades Boko Haram's Den. Re-

trieved   January   12,   2013   from
http://allafrica.com/stories/201206010222.html.

29. *Reuters* (March 30, 2011). Bomb scare disrupts opposition rally in NE Nigeria. Retrieved June 15, 2013 from http://www.reuters.com/article/2011/03/30/ozatp-nigeria-violence.

30. *UPI.Com* (March 30, 2011). More bombs follow Nigeria inauguration.   Retrieved   June   15,   2012   from http://www.upi.com/Top_News/World-News/2011/05/30/.

31. *Vanguard* (April 9, 2011). Bomb rocks polling center in Maiduguri.   Retrieved   June   15,   2012   from http://www.vanguardngr.com/2011/04/bomb-rocks-polling-centre-in-maiduguri/

32. Bloomberg (April 16, 2011). Nigeria Police Arrest Four After Election Day Blast, Shooting in Maiduguri, Retrieved June   15,   2012   from http://www.bloomberg.com/news/2011-04-16/nigeria-police-arrest-four-after-election-day-blast-shooting-in-maiduguri.html

33. Ibid

34. http://www.google.com/hostednews/canadianpress/article/ ALeqM5gc   TuVy16m43   uhuVJ66ZY SjXPa8qQ?docId=6632501

35. *This Day* (April 23, 2011). Boko Haram Raids Yola Prison, Frees 14. Retrieved June 20, 2012 from
http://www.thisdaylive.com/articles/boko-haram-raids-yola-prison-frees-14/90140/.

36. UPI.Com (May 30, 2011). More bombs follow Nigeria inauguration.   Retrieved   June   15,   2012   from http://www.upi.com/Top_News/World-News/2011/05/30/.

37. Ibid.

38. Ibid.

39. Ibid.

40. *Vanguard* (June 1, 2012) Nigeria: Kidnapped German, Six Gunmen Killed as JTF Invades Boko Haram's Den. Re-

trieved January 12, 2013 from http://allafrica.com/stories/ 201206 010222.

41. BBC News Africa (June 7, 2011). 'Boko Haram' gunmen kill Nigerian Muslim cleric Birkuti. Retrieved July 20, 2013 from http://www.bbc.co.uk/news/world-africa-13679234

42. Reuters.com (June 17, 2011) Nigerian Islamist sect claims bomb attack. Retrieved June 20, 2012 from http://www.reuters.com/article/2011/06/17/ozatp-nigeria-bomb/.

43. *Reuters* (June 26, 2011). Update 1-Bomb kills 25 at Nigerian drinking spot – sources. Retrieved May 12, 2012 from http://www.reuters.com/article /2011/06/ 26/nigeria-blasts/.

44. Saharareporters.com (July 10, 2011). Bomb Blast in Suleija, Niger State Kills Three. Retrieved June 15, 2012 from http://saharareporters.com/news-page/bomb-blast-suleija-niger-state-kills-three.

45. Saharareporters.com (July 11, 2011). University Of Maiduguri Shut Down As Boko Haram-Linked Killings Increase. Retrieved June 30, 2012 from http://saharareporters.com/news-page/university-maiduguri-shut-down-boko-haram-linked-killings-increase

46. BBC News Africa (August 26, 2011). Abuja attack: Car bomb hits Nigeria UN building. Retrieved June 30, 2012 from http://www.bbc.co.uk/news/world-africa-14677957.

47. BBC News Africa (November 5, 2011). Nigeria Boko Haram attack 'kills 63' in Damaturu. Retrieved June 30, 2012 from http://www.bbc.co.uk/news/world-africa-15605041.

48. BBC News Africa (December 25, 2011). Nigeria churches hit by blasts during Christmas prayers. Retrieved June 10, 2012 from http://www.bbc.co.uk/news/world-africa-16328940

49. AL Jazeera (December 25, 2011). Scores killed in Nigeria clashes - Days of battles between Boko Haram and security forces leave more than 60 people dead near Maiduguri and Damaturu. Retrieved July 15, 2013. http://www.aljazeera.com/news/africa/2011/12/2011.htm

50. New York Times (December 26, 2011). Nigeria Arrests 2 in Blast That Killed 26 in Church. February 15, 2012. http://www.nytimes.com/2011/12/27/world/africa/nigeria-bombing-suspects-arrested.html?_r=2

51. *Leadership* (December 30, 2011). Nigeria: Smoke Out Boko Haram Sponsors, Jonathan Orders Security Chiefs. . Retrieved January 30, 2012 from http://allafrica.com/stories/201112300822.html.

52. *Reuters* (January 7, 2012). Christians flee attacks in northeast Nigeria. Retrieved June 20, 2012 from http://www.trust.org/item/?map=christians-flee-attacks-in-northeast-nigeria/.

53. Ibid.

54. Ibid.

55. Ibid.

56. Ibid.

57. Ibid.

58. *Vanguard* (January 9, 2012). President Jonathan's bombshell- "Boko Haram members are in my Government!" Retrieved May 25, 2012. http://www.vanguardngr. com/Pres-Jonathan's-bombshell-Boko-Haram-members- are –in- my- Government/

59. *Daily Trust* (January 12, 2012). Gunmen kill 4 travelers in Potiskum," Retrieved June 10, 2012 from http://dailytrust.com.ng/ index.php?option =com_content&view =article&id=152240:gunmen-kill-4-travellers- in-potiskum/

60. Human Rights Watch Report, October 2012) See also Boko Haram Suicide. Retrieved September 20, 2013 from http://www.longwarjournal. org/ archives/2012/11/ boko_haram_suicide_b.ph.

61. *Daily Trust* (January 23, 2012). Indian, Nepalese killed in Kano blasts. Retrieved September 5, 2012 from http://www.dailytrust.com.mg/index.Php? Option=com-contentand view=article&id=152914; indian--napalese-killed-in-kano-blasts.

62. Reuters (January 28, 2012). Nigeria army says kills 11 Boko Haram insurgents. Retrieved February 18, 2012 from http://www.reuters.com/article /2012/01/28/us-nigeria-violence/

63. Daily Trust (March 30, 2012). Four dead, Boko Haram claims responsibility. Retrieved September 20, 2012 from http://www.allafrica.com/stories /2012033003-46.html.

64. Pilot Africa (October 22, 2012).Boko Haram killed Cameroonian mayor, newspaper claims. Retrieved December 18, 2012 from http://www. pilot africa. com/2012/10/22/boko-haram-killed- Cameroonian-mayor-newspaper-claims/. See also http://sunnewsonline.com/new/national/boko-haram-kills-cameroon-mayor/

65. Reuters (January 21, 2012). Nigerian sect kills over 100 in deadliest strike yet. Retrieved June 25, 2012 from http://www.reuters.com/article/2012 /01/21/us-nigeria-blast/

66. BBC News Africa (February 8, 2012) Nigeria: Boko Haram claims Kaduna army suicide attack, Retrieved January 20, 2013 from http://www.bbc .co.uk/news/world-africa-16942694.

67. Ibid.

68. The Guardian (March 19, 2012). Car explodes near Nigeria's capital, wounds 1. Retrieved September 20, 2013 from http://www.guardian. co.uk/world/ feedarticle/

69. Longwarjournal.com (Feb. 2012). Retrieved June 20, 2012 from http://www.longwarjournal.org/ threat-matrix/archives/2012/02/boko_haram_suicide _ bomber_kill.php.

70. Daily Mail (March 9, 2013). British hostage is feared to have been executed by Nigerian terrorists who panicked after local media said 'UK warplanes were in the area preparing for a rescue bid.' Retrieved July 20, 2013 from http://www.daily mail. co.uk/news/ article-2290732/British-Hostage -feared-executed-Nigerian-terrorists- panicked-

local-media-said-UK-warplanes-area-   preparing-rescue-
bid.html/. See also Human Rights Watch Report, October
2012.

71. *Vanguard* (March 11, 2012). Suicide Bomber Kills 3 –
Others Injured in Jos Church. Retrieved June 18, 2013 from
http://www.vanguardngr.com/   2012/03/suicide-bomber-
killed-3-others-injured-in-jos-church/

72. *Vanguard* (April 9, 2013). Easter Tragedies: 58 die in bomb
blast, church collapse. Retrieved June 18, 2013 from
http://www.vanguardngr.com /2012/04/easter-tragedies-58-
die-in-bomb-blast-church-collapse/.

73. *Vanguard* (April 26, 2013). ThisDay's editorial board
chairman confirms suicide attack. Retrieved June 18, 2013
from http://www.vanguardngr.com/2012/04/this days- edi-
torial- board-chairman-confirms-suicide-attack/

74. BBC News Africa (April 30, 2012). Deadly attack on Nigeria's Bayero University in Kano. Retrieved June 20,
2013   from   http://www.bbc.co.uk/news/world-africa-
17886143

75. Ibid.

76. *Vanguard* (April 30, 2013). Suicide bomber assails Police
boss convoy, kills 11. Retrieved June 4, 013.
http://www.vanguardngr.com/2012/04/suicide-bomber-
assails-police-boss-convoy- kills-11/

77. Associated Press (June 12, 2012) Al-Qaeda blames Germany for Nigeria hostage death. See also Human Rights
Watch Report, October 2012. Retrieved July 8, 2013 from
http://www.longwarjournal   .org/   threat-matrix
/archives/2012/06/ suicide bomber kills_15_ at_nig.php.

78. Ibid.

79. Vanguard (June 4, 2012). Nigeria: Bauchi Church Bombings - Boko Haram Claims Responsibility. Retrieved July 8,
2013 from http://allafrica.com/stories/ 201206050 439.htm.

80. Roggio Bill (November 25, 2012). Boko Haram Suicide
Bombs Kill 11at Nigeria Military Church. *The Long Jour-*

nal. Retrieved July 8, 2013 from http://www. longwarjournal.org/archives/2012/11/boko_haram _suicide_b.php

81. News2.onlinenigeria.com (July 11, 2012). Boko Haram Kills 130 Innocent Villagers In Plateau State. Retrieved January 9, 2013 from http://news2.onlinenigeria.com/ news/top-stories/177868-boko-haram-kills-130- innocent-villagers-in-plateau-state.html

82. Suicide Bomber Kills 5. *Longwarjournal* Retrieved June 17, 2013 from http://www.longwarjournal.org/threat-matrix/archives/2012/07 /suicide_ bomber_ kills_5_at_nige.php.

83. Human Rights Watch Report, October 2012.

84. BBC News Africa (June 18, 2012), Nigeria's Boko Haram 'bombed Kaduna churches.' Retrieved June 14, 2013 from http://www.bbc.co.uk/news/ world-africa-18496285.

85. Huffingtonpost.com (June 24, 2012). Boko Haram Prison Break: Radical Sect Frees 40 In Nigeria. Retrieved June 18, 2013 from http://www.huffingtonpost. com/2012/06/25/boko-haram-prison-break_n_ 1624339.html.

86. *Reuters* (July 26, 2012), Suspected members of Boko Haram kill two Indians. Retrieved August 1, 2013 from http://www.reuters.com/article/2012/07/26/us-nigeria-bokoharam/

87. Vanguard (August 3, 2012). Emir's bodyguard, mosque aide hurt in suicide attack in Potiskum. Retrieved January 10, 2013 from http://www.vanguard ngr.com /2012/08/ emirs-bodyguard-mosque-aid-hurt-in-suicide-attack-in-potiskum/. See also http://www.vanguardngr.com /2012/07/sokoto-suicide-bomber-kills-self-police-officer/

88. Ibid.

89. The Hindu (August 8, 2012). 19 dead in Nigeria church attack. Retrieved October 10, 2013 from
http://www.thehindu.com/news/international/articl e3738891. See also http://www.thenews.com.pk/ Article- 62139-Bomb- kills-5-soldiers-in-Nigeria/

90. Vanguard (August15, 2012) Four Killed and 3 Injured in a Failed Suicide Attempt. Retrieved October 20, 2013 from http://www.vanguardngr. com/ 2012/08/four-killed-3-injured-in-failed- suicide- attempt/

91. Reuters (September 17, 2012) Nigeria Troops Kill Boko Haram Spokesman – Source. Retrieved January 30, 2013 from http://www.reuters.com/article/2012/09/17/us-nigeria-bokoharam-id/

92. Al-Jazeera (September 23, 2012). Suicide bomber strikes church in Nigeria. Retrieved July 20, 2013 from http://www. aljazeera.com /news/africa /2012/09/2012.html. Also available at http://www.vanguardngr.com /2012 /09/ two-killed- many-wounded-as-suicide-bomber-hits-church/

93. News2 online.com (October 3, 2012). Boko Haram Kills 130 Innocent Villagers in Plateau State". News2.onlinenigeria.com. Retrieved July 13, 2012.

94. Nigeriavillagers.com (October 28, 2012). Catholic Church bombed in Kaduna. Retrieved July 20, 2012 from http://www.nigeriavillagesquare.com / forum/main-square/73727-suicide-bomber-strikes-kaduna-church.html. See also http://www.vanguard ngr.com /2012/09/two-killed-many- wounded-as-suicide-bomber-hits-church/.

95. Boko Haram suicide bombs kill 11 at Nigerian military church. Retrieved July 20, 2012. Retrieved July 20, 2013 from http://www.longwar journal.org/ ar-chives/2012/11/boko_haram_suicide_b.php.

96. Reuters (June 17, 2012) Fact box on recent Boko Haram strikes on Nigerian churches. Retrieved July 20, 2012 from http://www.reuters.com/ /article/ 2012/06/17/us-nigeria-violence-churches-i/.

97. CNK Nigeria.Com. (May 25, 2013). How Boko Haram Killed 4 Ibadan Traders. Retrieved June 8, 2013 from http://www.ckn nigeria.com/ 2013/05/how-boko-haram-killed-4-ibadan-traders.html.

98. Ibid. See also http://www.reuters.com/article/2012 /06/17/us-nigeria-violence-churches-i/.

99. Al-Jazeera (May 18, 2013). Nigeria sets curfew in Boko Haram stronghold Residents of Maiduguri ordered to stay indoors as military launches strikes against armed group in the north. Retrieved July 20, 2013 from http://www.aljazeera.com/ news/africa/2013/05/2013 5181431 5995937.html

100. Al-Jazeera (May 17, 2013). Nigerian forces 'shell fighter camps' - At least 21people killed in Bornu state as army launches offensive against Boko Haram strongholds in the northeast. Retrieved July 18, 2013 from http://www. Aljazeera/news/africa/2013/ 05/2013517116303 7848.html.

101. Human Rights Watch Report, October 2012.

102. Ibid.

103. Ibid.

104. *Reuters* (May 29, 2013). Boko Haram rebels say Nigerian military offensive is failing. Retrieved July 7, 2013 from http://www.tvcnews.tv /?q=article/ boko-haram-rebels-say-nigerian-military-offensive-failing-reuters/

105. BBC News Africa (June 4, 2013). United States offer rewards for capture of African militants. Retrieved July 20, 2013from
   http://www.bbc .co.uk/ news/world-africa- 22763305.See also AFP (June 3, 2013 at http://www.vanguardngr.com/ 2013/06/united -states-places-23-million-reward-for-shekur-4-others.

106. *Premium Times* (June 5, 2013). Boko Haram members flee to Niger as Nigerian military arrest 55 terrorists in Yobe, Bornu. Retrieved July 20, 2013 from http://premiumtimesng.com /news/137706-boko-haram-members-flee-to- niger-as-nigerian-military-arrest-55-terrorists-in-yobe-Bornu.html..

107. WorldNews on NBC TV USA (July 6, 2013). 29 boarding school students burned alive, shot dead by Islamist militants in Nigeria. Retrieved July 20, 2013 from

http://worldnews. nbcnews.com/ _news /2013/ 07/06/ 19318588-29- boarding-school-students-burned-alive-shot-dead-by-islamistmilitants-in-nigeria?lite.

108.	AFP (July 7, 2013) Nigeria school attack claims 42 lives. Retrieved July 20 2013 from http://www.theaustralian.com. au/news/world/ nigeria-school-attack-claims-42-lives/story-e6frg6so-1226675417375

109.	*Leadership* (July 10, 2013). Nigeria: Four Boko Haram Members Get Life Sentence. Retrieved July 21, 2013. http://allafrica.com/stories/201307100752.html.

110.	News2.online (June 27, 2013). I killed 23 people in 2 days, Boko Haram member confesses. Retrieved July 20, 2013 from http://news2.onlinenigeria.com/news/crime/299667-i-killed-23-people-in-2-days-boko-haram-member- confesses.html

111.	CKN Nigeria.com (July 15, 2013). Boko Haram Shallow Graves, Arms Bunker Discovered In Maiduguri. Retrieved July 20, 2013 from http://www.cknnigeria.com/2013/07/boko-haram-shallow-gravesarms-bunker. html/

112.	Vanguard (July 16, 2013). Boko Haram ceasefire: Operation continues until... – Army. Retrieved July 20, 2013 from http://www.vanguardngr.com /2013/07/boko- haram-ceasefire-operation-continues-until-army/

113.	Early Hours Attack: Gunmen Killed By Locals in Southern ... (n.d.). Retrieved from http://news.naij.com/40808.html

114.	Saharareporters.com (July 21, 2013). Indigenes Repels Attacks, Kill Five Gunmen in Southern Kaduna. Retrieved July 21, 2013 from http://saharareporters.com /news-page/indigenes-repels-attacks-kill-five-gunmen-southern-kaduna/

115.	*Vanguard* (July 30, 2013). Army arrests 42 Boko Haram Members. Retrieved August 6, 2013 from http://www.vanguardngr. com /2013/07/army-arrests-42-boko-haram-members/. Retrieved August 6, 2013.

116.   NaijaPundit.com (August 2, 2013). Coup in Boko Haram as Shekau is Toppled by His Lieutenants. Retrieved, August 3, 2013. http://www.naijapun dit.com /news/ coup-in-boko-haram-as-shekau-is-toppled-by-his-lieutenants.

117.   Vanguard (August 5, 2013). 35 killed as Boko Haram, JTF clash. Retrieved August 5, 2013 from http://www.vanguard ngr.com /2013/08/35- killed-as-boko-haram-jtf-clash/

118.   Saharareproters.com (August 6, 2013). International Criminal Court Indicts Boko Haram For Crimes Against Humanity. Retrieved August 8, 2013.

119.   Vanguard (August 12, 2013). 44 worshippers shot dead in Borno mosque. Retrieved August 13, 2013 from http://www.vanguardngr.com/ 2013 /08/44-worshippers-shot-dead-in-borno-mosque/

120.   Saharareporters.com (August 13, 2013). Boko Haram Leader Pokes Fun At US, France, Claims Sect Winning War Against Nigerian Military-Premium Times. Retrieved August 14, 2013 from http://saharareporters.com/news-page/boko-haram-leader- pokes-fun-us-france-claims-sect-winning-war-against-nigerian-military/

121.   Sahararporters.com (August 14, 2013). h Retrieved August 16, 2013 from htp://saharareporters.com/news-page/nigerian-troops-kill-boko-haram-second-command-abu-saad/

122.   Sahararporters.com (August 16, 2013). Security Jitters over Emergence of Another Islamic Sect in Northern Nigeria, As Boko Haram Threatens Kebbi. Retrieved August 17, 2013 from http://saharareport ers.com/news-page/ security-jitters-over-emergence-another   -Islamic-sect-northern-nigeria-boko-haram-threatens/

123.   BBC News Africa (August 16, 2013). Nigeria unrest: 'Boko Haram' in deadly attack on Damboa. Retrieved August 17, 2013 from http://www.bbc.co. uk/news/world-africa-23736053.

124. Irporterstv.com (August 19, 2013). Shekau, Boko Haram Leader Dies of Gunshot Wounds. http://ireporterstv.co/shekau-boko-haram-leader-dies-of-gunshot-wounds/. Also see CNN World Report (August 19, 2013). Nigerian army says it killed No. 2 leader of extremist group Boko Haram. Retrieved August 19, 2013 from http://www.cnn. com/2013 /08/15/ world/africa/nigeria-boko-haram-commander-killed/index.html?iref=allsearch.Vanguard (august 19, 2013).Retrieved August 19, 2013 from http://www.vanguardngr.com/2013/08/boko-haram- chief-who-again- may-be-dead/

125. Vanguard (August 23, 2013). Boko Haram kills 35 in Borno village attack. Retrieved August 25, 2013 from http://www.vanguardngr. com/2013/08/ boko-haram-kills-35-in-borno-village-attack/

126. The Daily Trust (August 22, 2013). 13 killed in separate attacks in Borno. Retrieved August 22, 2013 from http://dailytrust.info/index. Php/news/3769-13 -killed-in-separate-attacks-in-borno.

127. African Spotlight (August 27, 2013). Boko Haram dressed as soldiers kill 14 vigilantes in Bama. Retrieved August 27, 2013 from tttp://www.africans potlight. com/2013/08/27/boko-haram-dressed-as-soldiers-kill-14-vigilantes-in-bama/

128. Vanguard (August 31, 2013). 54 killed, 36 missing in Borno Boko Haram attacks. Retrieved August 31, 2013 from http://www.vanguardngr. com/2013/08/54-killed-36-missing-in-brono-boko-haram-attacks/.

129. Vanguard (September 7, 2013). 50 killed in air strike on Boko Haram camps in Borno. Retrieved September 9, 2013 from http://. www vanguardngr. com/2013/09/50-killed-in-air-strike-on-boko-haram-camps-in-borno/

130. The Punch (September 8, 2013). CAN hails JTF for tackling Boko. Haram. Retrieved September 8, 2013 from

http://www.punchng.com/news/can- hails-jtf- for-tackling-boko-haram/

131.   September 16, 2013. Nigerian soldiers linked to Boko Haram get death penalty and jail terms. Retrieved September 26, 2013 from http://sunnewsonline.net/news/18-nigerian-soldiers-linked-with-boko-haram-gets-death-jail-terms

132.   Premium Times (September 17, 2013). 40 Soldiers Killed, 65 Missing In Fresh Boko Haram Ambush. Retrieved September 18, 2013. From http://saharareporters.com/ news-page/exclusive-40-soldiers -killed-65-missing-fresh-boko-haram-ambush-premium-times.

133.   *Africanspotlight* (September 20, 2013). 8 killed as Boko Haram members in Army uniform attack Abuja legislative quarters. Retrieved September 20, 2013 from http://www.africanspotlight.com /2013/ 09/20/8 -killed-as-boko-haram-members-in-army-uniform-attack-abuja-legislative-quarters/.

134.   CKN online Newsmagazine (September 20, 2013). 142 Corpses Recovered After Boko Haram Highway Massacre. Retrieved September 20, 2013 from http://www.cknnigeria.com/2013/09/142-corpes-recovered-after-boko-haram.html.

135.   *Vanguard* (September 26, 2013). I am alive, says Abubakar Shekau in new video. Retrieved September 26, 2013 from http://www.vanguardngr .com/2013/09/i-am-alive-says-abubakar-shekau-in-new-video/

136.   *Africanspotlight* (September 26, 2013). Boko Haram Islamists open fire in church, kill Pastor and his 2 children. RetrievedSeptember26,2013http://www.africanspotlight.com/2013/09/26/boko-haram-islamists-open-fire-in-church-kill-pastor-and-his-2-children/

137.   *Associated Press* (September 29, 2013). Nigeria: Militants kill students in college attack. http://news.yahoo.com/nigeria-militants-kill-students-

college-attack-095734028.html. See also Vanguard (September 29, 2013). Death toll in Yobe college attack rises to 40. Retrieved September 29, 2013 from http://www.vanguardngr .com/ 2013/09/death-toll-yobe-college-attack-rises-40/

138. *CKN Nigeria* (September 30, 2013). Yobe Students Attack - Death Toll Rises to 78. Retrieved October 8, 2013 from http://www. cknnigeria.com/ 2013/09/yobe-students-attackdeath-toll-rises-to.html.

139. *CKN Nigeria* (September 30, 2013). Boko Haram Beheads Seven People, Slit Another Four Throats. Retrieved September 30, 2013 from http://www. cknnigeria.com/2013/09/boko-haram-beheads-seven-   peopleslit.html.

140. *The Nation* (October 4, 2013). Military kills scores in Boko Haram Yobe air raid. Retrieved October 5, 2013 from http://thenationonlineng.net   /new/military-kills-scores-in-boko-haram-yobe-air-raid/. The Nation reported that between July & September 2013, about 80 school children were killed by unknown gun men in two separate attacks in Yobe State. On July 30, 2013 according to the Nation, 30 pupils (this is not here on the timeline for this book), 30 people including 25 school children were killed in their dormitories in Mamudo, Yobe State.

141. IReportersTv.com (October 26, 2013). 74 suspected Boko Haram Suspected Insurgents Killed by Nigerian Military. Retrieved October 28, 2013 from http://ireporterstv. co/74-suspected-boko-haram-insurgents   -killed-by-nigerian-military-borno-state.

142. IreporterTV.com (October 29, 2013).Boko Haram Kills 35 Nigerian Soldiers in Kano. Retrieved October 29, 2013. From http://ireporter stv. Co/boko-haram-kills-35-nigerian-soldiers-in-kano/? from=fb.

143. Boko Haram's Shekau in new video, claims leading Damaturu attack. Retrieved   November 3, 2013 from

http://www.africanspotlight.com/ 2013/11/03/boko-harams-shekau-in-new-video-claims-leading-damaturu-attack/

144.   Gunmen Kill Over 30 In Attack On Wedding Convoy Between Adamawa and Borno. Retrieved November 3, 2013 from http://saharareporters.com/ news-page/gunmen-kill-over-30-attack-wedding-convoy-between-adamawa-and-borno/

145.   AFP (November 4, 2013). 70 Boko Haram members kill 40 people, burn 300 homes. Retrieved on November 4, 2013   from   http://www. africanspotlight.com/2013/11/04/70-boko-haram-members-kill-40-people-burn-300-homes/.

146.   *Saharareporters.com* (November 9, 2013). In Kano, Two Soldiers Killed In Shootout With Boko Haram. Retrieved   on   November   10,   2013   from http://saharareporters.com/news-page/kano-two-soldiers-killed-shootout-boko-haram.

147.   *Los Angeles Times* (November 13, 2013). 2 Nigerian groups added to U.S. list of terrorist organizations. Retrieved   November   16,   2013   from http://www.latimes.com/world/la-fg-boko-haram.

148.   *PM News* (November 15, 2013). Boko Haram ThisDay Bomber Jailed For Life. Retrieved November 16, 2013 from   http://www.   http://   saharareporters.com/news-page/boko-haram-thisday-bomber-jailed-life-pm-news-lagos.

149.   Africvilla.com (November 18, 2013). Escaped French Hostage Arrives Home from Nigeria. Retrieved November 18, 2013 from http://africvilla.com/index.php/africa2/10-nigeria/293-escaped-french-hostage-arrives-home-from-nigeria/

150.   Vanguard (November 19, 2013). Multiple explosions, gun battle rock Kano. Retrieved November 19, 2013 from http://www.vanguard ngr. com /2013/11/ multiple-explosions-gun-battle-rock-kano/.

151. Vanguard (November 20, 2013). DSS parades varsity don who recruits for Boko Haram. Retrieved November 20, 2013 from http://www.vanguard ngr. com /2013/11/dss-parade-varsity-don-recruits-boko-haram/

152. *ThisDay* (November 25, 2013). ICC Declares Conflict in N'Eastern Nigeria Civil War. Retrieved November 26, 2013 from http://www.thisdaylive. com/articles/icc-declares-conflict-in-n-eastern-nigeria-civil-war/165171/.

153. Maiduguri International Airport closed after Boko Haram raided a nearly Air force Base. There was no report of casualties. It was gathered that more than 300 members of the terror group invaded the air force in a convoy of vans. Sahararporters.com (2013, December 2) Maiduguri International Airport Closed After Boko Haram Raid On Air Force Base. Retrieved December 2, 2013 from http://saharareporters.com/ news-page/maiduguri-international-airport-closed-after-boko-haram-raid-air-force-base.

154. Saharareporters.com (2013, December 20). Boko Haram – St Theresa Catholic Church Christmas Bomber Kabiru Sokoto Gets Life Imprisonment. Retrieved December 21, 2013 from http://saharareporters.com/ news-page/boko-haram-st-theresa-catholic-church-christmas-bomber-kabiru-sokoto-gets-life-imprisonment/

155. Saharareporters.com (2013, December 20). Boko Haram attacks Bama Army Barracks in Bornu State, Women and Children Killed. Retrieved December 21, 2013 from http://saharareporters.com/news-page/boko-haram-attacks-bama-army-barracks-bornu-state-women-and-children-killed/

156. Saharareporters.com (2013, December 24). Boko Haram Killed 15 Soldiers in Borno. Nigeria Military Admits Nigeria's military disclosed it lost 15 members of the armed forces during December 20, 2013 attack by the militant Boko Haram Islamic sect in Bama, Borno State. Over

50 members of Boko Haram members were killed in the attack, and over 20 vehicles belonging to the terror group destroyed. Retrieved December 24, 2013 from http://saharareporters.com/news-page/boko-haram-killed-15-soldiers-borno-nigeria-military-admits.

157.   Saharareporters.com (2013, December 24). Churches Cancel Christmas Night Services in Borno, and Yobe States as a precaution against Boko Haram's violence. Retrieved December 24, 2013 from http://saharareporters.com/news-page/churches-cancel-christmas-night-services-borno-yobe-states/

158.   Cknnigeria.com (2014, January 3). Boko Haram Release Kidnapped French Priest Retrieved January 3, 2014 from http://www.cknnigeria .com/2014/01/ boko-haram-release-kidnapped-french.html.

159.   The Christian Science Monitor (2013, January 28, 2014). Nigerians call for new strategy after Boko Haram strikes yet again - A state of emergency and a full-scale military offensive have not stopped horrific Boko Haram attacks in Nigeria. Retrieved January 28, 2014 from http://news.yahoo.com/nigerians-call-strategy-boko-haram-strikes-yet-again-140628461.html.

160.   Saharareporters.com (2014, January 29). Adamawa Bishop Says Boko Haram Killed 31 Of His Parishioners And Injured 11. Retrieved January 30, 2014 from http://saharareporters.com/news-page/adamawa-bishop-says-boko-haram-killed-31-his-parishioners-and-injured-11.

161.   AFP (2014, February 5). 'Do not disappoint', Nigeria's new top brass told. Retrieved February 6, 2014 from http://news.yahoo.com/39-not-disappoint-39-nigeria-39-top-brass-194149802.html.

162.   Associated Press (AP) (2013 February 5, 2014. Extremists attack in northeast Nigerian town kills 39. Retrieved February 16, 2014 from http://news.yahoo. com/extremists-attack-northeast-nigerian-town-kill-39-144954690.html.

163.   AFP (2014, February 15). Hundreds flee north Nigeria town fearing attack. Retrieved February 16, 2014 from http://news.yahoo.com/hundreds-flee-north-nigeria-town-fearing-attack-184958780.html.

164.   Daily Trust (2014, February 25). Boko Haram Gunmen Kill 40 Students at Federal Govt. College in Yobe. Retrieved February 26, 2014 from http://saharareporters.com/news-page/boko-haram-gunmen-kill-40-students-federal-govt-college-yobe-dailytrust-newspaper.

165.   Associated Press (2014, March 2). 90 killed in two attacks in northern Nigeria. Twin car bombs exploded in a bustling marketplace in Maiduguri on March 2, killing more than 50 people. The victims were children dancing at a wedding celebration and people watching a soccer match at a cinema. In a Mainok village, 60 kilometers (40 miles) away, suspected extremists also struck Saturday night, killing 39 people. Retrieved March 14, 2014 from http://news.yahoo.com/90-killed-2-attacks-northern-nigeria-162751001.html.

166.   Politicaleconomistng.com (2014, March 4). Boko Haram: 600 Killed In Two Months—-Amnesty International. Retrieved March 15, 2014 from http: // www. political economistng.com/boko-haram-600-killed-in-two-months-amnesty-international/.

167.   AP (2014, March 14). Suspected extremists attack northern Nigeria city, this time Military Barracks in the capital city of Maiduguri, the base of the Islamic terror group. The jihadists fought their way into the military barracks and freed several militants detained in cells at the barracks. Reports indicated that Boko Haram members released were shot as they attempted to escape from the military barracks. Retrieved March 14, 2014 from http://news.yahoo.com/ suspected-extremists-attack-northern-nigeria-city-082243848.html.

168.   AP (2014 April 14). Blast rips up busy bus station in Nigerian capital. Retrieved April 14, 2014 from http://news.yahoo.com/blast-rips-busy-bus-station-nigerian-capital-082718610.html. See similar story on Saharareporters.com on http://saharareporters.com/ news-page/abuja-bus-station-bombing-update.

169.   Reuters (2014, April 13). Nigeria Islamists kill 68 in two village attacks: witnesses. Retrieved April 15, 2014 from http://news.yahoo.com/nigeria-islamists-kill-68-two-village-attacks-witnesses-224545665.html?soc_src=mediacontentstory.

170.   Reuters (2014, April 15) Suspected Islamist rebels abduct over 100 Nigerian schoolgirls: teacher. Retrieved April 16, 2014 from http://news.yahoo.com/ suspected-islamist-rebels-abduct-over-100-nigeria-schoolgirls-151249139.html.

171.   CNN (2014, April 16). Nigerian military: Over 100 girls abducted from school are freed, 8 still missing. Retrieved April 16, 2014 from http://www.cnn.com/2014/04/16/world/africa/nigeria-girls-abducted.

172.   NPR (2014, May 2, 2014) Fate of Kidnapped Nigerian School Girls Remains Unknown. Retrieved May 5, 2014 from http://www.npr.org/2014/05/02/ 308899237/fate-of-kidnapped-nigerian-school-girls-remains-unknown.

173.   Bloomberg News (2014, May 3). Nigerian President Orders Probe into Schoolgirls' Kidnapping. Retrieved May 5, 2014 from http://www.bloomberg. com/news/2014-05-03/nigerian-president-orders-probe-into-schoolgirls-kidnapping.html.

174.   Fox News (2014, May 4). Kerry: US will aid in hunt for kidnapped Nigerian schoolgirls. Retrieved May 5, 2014 from http://www.foxnews.com/politics/ 2014/05/04/kerry-us-will-aid-in-hunt-for-kidnapped-nigerian-schoolgirls/.

175.   The African Examiner (May 4, 2014). Boko Haram Kills 10 of the abducted Girls of Chibok. retrieved May 5, 2014 from http://www. africanexaminer.com/

176.   CNN (May 5, 2014). I will sell them,' Boko Haram leader says of kidnapped Nigerian girls. Retrieved May 5, 2014 from http://www.cnn.com/ 2014/05/05/world/africa/nigeria-abducted-girls/. See also The Guardian, (May 5, 2014) Boko Haram claims responsibility for kidnapping Nigeria schoolgirls http://www.theguardian.com/world/2014/ may/05/boko-haram-claims-responsibility-kidnapping -nigeria-schoolgirls. See also NBC Nightly News with Brian Williams. (May 5, 2014). Missing Nigeria Schoolgirls. http://www.nbcnews.com/storyline/ missing-nigeria-schoolgirls/nigerian-girls-kidnapper-sends-chilling-message-n97636

177.   Time (2012, May 2014). Boko Haram Abducted 8 More Girls in Nigeria, Police Say. Retrieved May 6, 2014 from http://time.com/89352/boko-haram-nigeria-abduction/ Also at BBC (March 6, 2014) More Nigerian girls abducted by suspected Boko Haram militants. http://www.bbc.com/news/world-africa-27298614.

178.   Washington Post (2014, May 6, 2014) Obama: US to help Nigeria find kidnapped girls. Retrieved May 6, 2014 from http://www.washingtonpost.com/politics /courts_law/us-team-to-help-nigeria-locate-kidnapped-girls/

179.   Punch (2014, May 10). Schoolgirls: American, British experts arrive Nigeria Retrieved May 10, 2014 from http://www.punchng.com/ news/ schoolgirls-american-british-experts-arrive-nigeria/

180.   Associated Press (2013, May 10). First lady gives weekly address on Nigerian girls. Retrieved May 10, 2014 from http://news.yahoo.com/first-lady-gives-weekly-address-nigerian-girls-101142983.html.

181.   AFP (2014, May 12). New Boko Haram video claims to show missing Nigerian schoolgirls. Retrieved May 12, 2014 from http://news.yahoo.com/ boko-haram-video-claims-show-missing-nigerian-schoolgirls-092349687.html.

182. The Independent (2014, May 16). The British face of Boko Haram: Man suspected of masterminding bomb attacks in Nigeria was radicalized at a Welsh university Retrieved May 16, 2014 from http://www.independent.co.uk/news/uk/crime/the-british-face-of-boko-haram-man-suspected-of-masterminding-bomb-attacks-in-nigeria-was-radicalised-in-glamorgan-9388373.html.

6. Boko Haram - Negotiating Amnesty Amidst Spiraling Violence & Deaths.

1.   Human Rights Report (October, 2012). Spiraling Violence.

2.   Ibid.

3.   Ibid.

4.   *Vanguard* (November 25, 2011). We are on a revenge mission, Boko Haram suspect tells the court. Retrieved September 10, 2012 from http://www.vanguardngr.Com/2011/11/we-are-on-revenge-mission-boko-haram-suspect-tells-court.

5.   *This Day* (September 22, 2010). Boko Haram claims killings in Borno. Retrieved September 30 from http://www.thiddaylive   /article/boko-haram-claims-killing-in-borno/78273.

6.   Human Rights Watch Report, October 2012.

7.   Human Rights Watch Report, October 2012. Sahara Reporters.com (May 22, 2013). Some Nigerian Soldiers Help Boko Haram – Lt. General Ihejirika. Retrieved July 30, 2013 from http://saharareporters.com /news-page/some-nigerian-soldiers-help-boko-haram-lt-general/.

8. Human Rights Watch Report, October 2012. The Nai-
   jaPundit.com (August 2, 2013). Coup in Boko Haram as
   Shekau is Toppled by His Lieutenants. Retrieved, August 3, 2013 from http://www.naija pundit.com/
   news/coup-in-boko-haram-as-Shekau-is-toppled-by-
   his's-lieutenants/

9. Human Rights Report – *Spiraling Violence*.

   October, 2012.
10. Ibid 19. See also Congressional Testimony by Assistant
    Secretary Johnnie Carson, US Department of State,
    House Foreign Affairs Committee, Subcommittee on
    African Affairs, "U.S. Policy Towards Nigeria: West
    Africa's Troubled Titan," July 10, 2012.

11. Ibid
12. Ibid
13. AP (2014 April 14). Blast rips up busy bus station in
    Nigerian capital. Retrieved April 14, 2014 from
    http://news.yahoo.com/blast-rips-busy-bus-station-
    nigerian-capital-082718610.html. See similar story on
    Saharareporters.com on http://saharareporters.com/
    news-page/abuja-bus-station-bombing-update
14. CNN (2014, February 20) Diplomatic talks in Ukraine
    last until dawn, a day after 100 may have died. Re-
    trieved April 2, 2014 from
    http://www.cnn.com/2014/02/20/world/europe/ukraine-
    protests/
15. *The Nation* (May 16, 2013). Nigeria continued violence
    worries UN Chief. Retrieved June 10, 2013 from
    http://www.thenationonlineeng.net/   news-
    update/nigeria-continue-violence-worries-un-chief/.

16. *Punch* (February 27, 2013). Poverty fuelling Boko
    Haram insurgency – Clinton. Retrieved June 20, 2013

from http://www.punchng.com/news/ poverty-fuelling-
boko-haram-insurgency-clinton/

7. OPINIONS ON GRANTING AMNESTY TO BOKO HARAM - VIEWS FROM EMINENT POLITICIANS, TRADITIONAL AND RELI-GIOUS LEADERS.

1. *Vanguard* (March 16, 2013). Boko Haram: Mixed reactions trail call for Amnesty. Retrieved April 4, 2013 from http://www.vanguardngr.com/2013/03/boko-haram-mixed-reactions-trail-call-for- amnesty/
2. *The Leadership* (2013, March 31). Matthew Hassan Kukah-Easter Message: Amnesty, Repentance, Forgiveness and

Reconciliation. Retrieved April 4, 2013 from
http://leadership.ng/nga/articles/51192/2013/03/31/easter_
message_amnesty_repentance_forgiveness_and
_reconciliation. html.

3. Ibid.
4. From Amnesty to Repentance |. (2013, March 31). Re-
    trieved April 4, 2013 from http://aworship.com/from-
    amnesty-to-repentance/
5. *Vanguard* (April 3, 2013). Boko Haram should repent,
    apologize before amnesty – Onaiyekan. Retrieved April 4,
    2013 from http://www.vanguardngr.com/2013/04/boko-
    haram-should-repent-apologise-before-amnesty-onaiyekan/.
6. Information Nigeria (April 1, 2013). Amnesty Call: Sultan
    Is Encouraging and Condoning Bloody Violence – Afe-
    nifere. Retrieved April 4, 2013 http://www.information
    ng.com/2013/03/amnesty-call-sultan-is-encouraging-and-
    condoning-bloody-violence-afenifere.html.
7. News Agency of Nigeria (NAN) (March 31, 2013). Amnes-
    ty For Boko Haram: Sultan Goofed – CAN. Retrieved April
    30, 2013 from http://www.informationng.com /2013/03/
    amnesty-for-boko-haram-sultan-goofed-can.html.
8. *Vanguard* (April 3, 2013). Anglican Bishop to Boko Ha-
    ram: Unmask before seeking amnesty. Retrieved April 11,
    2013 from http://www.vanguardngr.com/2013/04/anglican-
    bishop-to-boko-haram-unmask-before-seeking-amnesty/
9. *Vanguard* (April 10, 2013). Boko Haram amnesty: You're
    on suicide mission, Christians tell FG. Retrieved April 11,
    2013 from http://www.vang uardngr.com/2013/04/boko-
    haram-amnesty-you're-on-suicide-mission-christians-tell-
    fg/.
10. Ibid.
11. *Punch* (March 31, 2013) If I Was President, I Would Grant
    Amnesty to Boko Haram-Atiku. http://www.naijapundit
    .com/news/if-i-was-president-i-would-grant-amnesty-to-
    boko-haram-atiku.
12. Ibid.

13. *Vanguard* (March 31, 2013). President's Easter Message to Nigerians. See also Boko Haram are not Muslims (March 31, 2013). President Good luck Jonathan speaking in his Easter Holiday message to Nigerians. Retrieved April 11, 2013 from http://naijamayor.com/boko-haram-are-not-muslims-goodluck-jonathan/? fb_source=pubv1.

14. *Naija Pundit* (April 11, 2013). After Establishing Drone Base in Niger U.S. Now Says Boko Haram Insurgency will soon end. Retrieved April 11, 2013 from http://www.naijapundit.com/news/ after-establishing-drone-base-in-niger-u-s-now-says-boko-haram-insurgency-will-soon-end.

15. *The Leadership* (April 9, 2013). Nigeria: Northern Elders to Go's - Bring Boko Haram Members for Dialogue.
Retrieved April 11, 2013 from http://allafrica.com/stories/ 01304100195.html? page=2.

16. *Vanguard* (May 19, 2013). Rev. Jesse Jackson Backs Amnesty for Boko Haram. Retrieved May 26, 2013 from http://www.vanguardngr.com/2013/05/rev-jesse-jackson-backs-amnesty-for-boko-haram/.

17. *The Nation* (May 26, 2013). Boko Haram: US secretary of state Kerry meets Jonathan. Retrieved May 27, 2013 from http://thenationonlineng.net /new/news-update/boko-haram-us-secretary-of-state-kerry-meets-jonathan/.

18. Ibid

19. *Daily Trust* (April 3, 2013). Agree on amnesty for Boko Haram and I'll lead negotiations - Former governor of Abia State, Orji Uzor Kalu. Retrieved June 18, 2013 From http://dailytrust.com.ng/index.php/politics/53813-agree-on-amnesty-for-boko-haram-and-i-ll-lead-negotiations.

20. Ibid.

21. Information Nigeria (April 2, 2013). Boko Haram Begins Mass Recruitment. Retrieved May 12, 2013 from http://www.informationng.com/2013/04/boko-haram-begin-mass-recruitment.html.

22. Ibid.
23. Vanguard (April 4, 2013). Boko Haram is your baby, Buhari fires back at Jonathan. Retrieved April 5, 2013 from http://www.vanguardngr.com/2013/04/boko-haram-is-your-baby-buhari-fires-back-at-jonathan/.
24. Ibid.
25. Ibid.
26. African Spotlight (April 6, 2013). Jonathan, forgive Boko Haram Retrieved April 7, 2013 from Turai.http://africanspotlight.com/2013/04/jonathan-forgive-boko-haram-turai/
27. Ibid.
28. *Naija* (April 7, 2013). PDP, CAN, ACF Disagree On Amnesty For Boko Haram. Retrieved April 6, 2013 from http://news.naij.com/ 30126.html.
29. Ibid
30. Ibid
31. Ibid
32. *Vanguard* (April 21, 2013). Boko Haram Amnesty: Scratching the surface of a nation's festering sore. Retrieved April 24, 2013 from http://www.vanguardngr.com /2013/04/boko-haram-amnesty-scratching-the-surface-of-a-nations-festering- sore/.
33. *Vanguard* (April 8, 2013). We're yet to decide on amnesty – Boko Haram. Retrieved April 8, 2013 from http://www.vanguardngr.com/2013/04/we-re-yet-to-decide-on-amnesty-boko- haram/.
34. *Naija Pundit* (April 8, 2013). Boko Haram to FG We Reject Your Amnesty! Retrieved April 9, 2013 from http://www.naija pundit.com/news/boko-haram-to-fg-we-reject-your-amnesty.
35. *Vanguard* (April 10, 2013). Boko Haram amnesty: You're on suicide mission, Christians tell FG. Retrieved April 11, 2013 from http://www.vanguardngr.com/2013/04/boko-haram-amnesty-youre-on-suicide-mission-christians-tell-fg/

36. AFP (July 30, 2013). Nigeria bombs kill 24 in mainly Christian area. http://au.news.yahoo.com/world/a/-/world/18234403/nigeria-bombs-kill-24-in-mainly-christian-area/ . Retrieved August 5, 2013. See also Vanguard (August 5, 2013). 35 Killed as Boko Haram, JTF Clash. http://www.vanguardngr.com/2013/08/35- killed-as-boko-haram-jtf-clash/.

37. *Vanguard* (August 2, 2013). Turaki – Journalists at War of Words over Boko Haram Peace Committee's Findings). Retrieved, August 5, 2013 from http://www.vanguard ngr.com/2013/08/turaki-journalist-at-war-of-words -over-boko-haram-peace-committee's-finding.

38. Saharareporters.com (2013, August 3). There is Grand Design to Plunger Northern Nigeria into Deeper Crisis – Sultan. Retrieved August 3, 2013 from http://saharareporters .com/ news-page/there-grand-design-plunge-northern-nigeria-deeper-crises-sultan. See also There Is a Grand Design to Plunge Northern Nigeria Into ... (2013, August 3). http://www.nigeriasun.com/index.php/ sid/216165307/scat/8db1f72cde37faf3

39. Beebe, S. A., Beebe, S. J., & Ivy, D. K., (2013). *Communication: Principles for a lifetime* (5th ed.). Boston: Allyn and Bacon.

8. NIGERIA – SHADING THE IMAGE OF A FAILEDSTATE

1. *Vanguard* (April 12, 2013). Nigeria is a terrorist state – Gen Idada. Online at http://www.vanguardngr.com/2013/04/nigeria-is-a-terrorist-state-gen-idada/. Retrieved April 15, 2013

2. Ibid.

3. Ibid.

4. Pope Francis begs Boko Haram to free hostages (March 31, 2013) Retrieved April 5, 2013 from .http://www.xclusive nige-

ria.com/index.php/component/k2/item/492-pope-francis-begs-boko-haram-to-free-hostages.

5. Boko Haram are not Muslims (March 31, 2013). President Good luck Jonathan speaking in his Easter Holiday Message to Nigerians. Retrieved April 5, 2013 from http://naijamayor .com/boko-haram-are-not-muslims-goodluck-jonathan/?fb_source=pubv1.

6. *Sahara Reporters* (April 8, 2013). Give Boko Haram Amnesty, Save Nigeria From War and Military Intervention – Muslim Group. Retrieved April 14, 2013 from http://sahara report-ers.com/news-page/give-boko-haram-amnesty-save-nigeria-war- and-military-intervention- 93-muslim-group

7. *Xclusive Magazine* (April 8, 2013). Nigerians too timid for revolution – Amaechi. Retrieved April 12, 2013 from http://www.xclusivenigeria. com/index php/news-stories

9. TERRORISM & SECTARIAN VIOLENCE - A REFLECTION ON NIGERIA' S PAST, PRESENT & WAYS FORWARD

1. Lyman, Princeton N. & Morrison, J. Stephen (2004). The Terrorist Threat in Africa. *Foreign Affairs*, January/February, 2004. Retrieved May 9, 2013 from http://www.foreign **af-**fairs.com/articles/59534/princeton-n-lyman-and-j-stephen-morrison/ the-terrorist-threat-in-africa.

2. Ibid

3. Allen, J.L. (2013). The Catholic Church: What Everyone Needs to Know. Oxford University Press. New York. Associated Press (2012, February 17). "Underwear bomber Umar Farouk Abdul Mutallab sentenced to life in prison". Daily Mail (London). Retrieved August 18, 2013 from http://www. dai-lymail.co.uk /news/article-2102254/ Underwear-bomber-Umar-Farouk -Abdulmutallab- sentenced-life-prison.html.

4. *New York Times* (June 11, 2003). Ugandan's Key to White House: AIDS.
5. *This Day* (April 6, 2012). 51 Rocket Launchers uncovered in Gombe. Retrieved April 10, 2012 from http://allafrica.com /stories/ 201204060768.html.
6. *The Independent* (2014, August 26). Iraq crisis: Isis declares its territories a new Islamic state with 'restoration of caliphate' in Middle East. Retrieved August 26, 2014 from http://www.independent. co. uk/ news/world/ middle-east/isis-declares-new-islamic-state-in-middle-east-with-abu-bakr-albaghdadi-as-emir-removing-iraq-and-syria-from-its-name-9571374.html

AFTERTHOUGHTS

Boko Haram, Terrorism and the Global Community.

1. Africanspotlight.com (August 13, 2013). No match for me': Boko Haram leader challenges Obama, two other foreign powers in new video. Retrieved August14, 2013from http://www.africanspotlight. Com/2013/08/13/no-match-for-me-boko-haram-leader-challenges-obama-2-other-foreign-powers-in-new-video/

2. Saharareporters.com (August 13, 2013). Boko Haram Leader Pokes Fun at US, France, Claims Sect Winning War Against Nigerian Military-Premium Times Retrieved August 14, 2013 from http://saharareporters.com/news-page/boko-haram-leader-pokes-fun-us-france-claims-sect-winning-war-against-nigerian-military-premium times.

3. Mayer, Jane (2008) *The Bomb Dark Side*, Double-day. *See also* Al Qaeda operative, key to 1998 U.S. Embassy bombings killed in Somali. Retrieved June 18, 2013 from http://articles.latimes .com/2011/jun /12/ world/ la-fg-embassy-bombings-20110612.

- U.S. Secretary of State, Senator John Kerry – "The kidnapping of hundreds of children by Boko Haram is an unconscionable crime."

- *Pope Francis*: In his first Easter Mass celebration as the new Pontiff - Calls for Prayers for Nigeria.

- There are "External Powers" behind Boko Haram to destabilize Nigeria and affirm the "Failed State" status –Opinions on the Streets in Nigeria.

- Terrorism is most likely to take place in countries that are not delivering to their people – *President Barack Obama* at town-hall meeting in Soweto with African Youths (Nigerians and South Africans).

- There is a grand design to push the entire Northern Nigeria into a deeper crisis and by extension the Nigeria Federation –Sultan of Sokoto, Mohammadu Sa'ad Abubakar III & Leader of Nigeria Muslims.

- On Amnesty for Boko Haram Members – "l believe so much in non-violence. Non-violence does not mean fear, but courage and thinking, and it means the ability to figure it out and fight it out. You must have the ability to resolve conflict, and not fight aggressively. It must not resort into killing and being killed." - Rev. Jesse Jackson.

- Poverty remains the main drive for the attacks by Boko Haram. It needs to be addressed by strong local and federal government programs---"too much inequality" is capable of limiting growth and opportunities among the citizens of a country – President Bill Clinton on Boko Haram's violence.

www.ingramcontent.com/pod-product-compliance
Lightning Source LLC
Chambersburg PA
CBHW060842280326
41934CB00007B/891